Dante Alighieri, Thomas William Parsons, 1265-1321 Dante Alighieri

**The First Canticle**

Inferno of the Divine Comedy of Dante Alighieri

Dante Alighieri, Thomas William Parsons, 1265-1321 Dante Alighieri

**The First Canticle**
*Inferno of the Divine Comedy of Dante Alighieri*

ISBN/EAN: 9783744661898

Printed in Europe, USA, Canada, Australia, Japan

Cover: Foto ©Thomas Meinert / pixelio.de

More available books at **www.hansebooks.com**

THE

# FIRST CANTICLE

## Inferno

OF THE

# DIVINE COMEDY

OF

DANTE ALIGHIERI

TRANSLATED BY

THOMAS WILLIAM PARSONS

BOSTON
DE VRIES, IBARRA AND COMPANY
MDCCCLXVII

Entered according to Act of Congress in the year 1867 by

THOMAS WILLIAM PARSONS

In the Clerk's office of the District Court of the District of Massachusetts

CAMBRIDGE
PRESS OF JOHN WILSON AND SON

TO

ANNA PARSONS

AND

AUGUSTA BARNARD

I Dedicate this Work.

T. W. PARSONS.

# INFERNO.

## CANTO THE FIRST.

HALFWAY on our life's journey, in a wood,
   From the right path I found myself astray.
   Ah! to describe how dark it was, — how rude
That savage forest! chills me to this day:
Its bitter thought is almost death to me;
   Yet, having found some good there, I will tell
   Of other things which there I chanced to see:
But, how I came therein, I know not well;
For sleep had mastered me when first I went
   From the true way, abandoned to my woe;
   Till having reached the foot of an ascent
   Where this vale ended that appalled me so,
Looking on high, its shoulders I beheld
   Robed in the Planet's rays who guides men right
   Through every pass: then part the fear was quelled
That froze my heart's lake all that piteous night.

Like one cast breathless, gasping from the spray,
  Who eyes the watery peril from the shore,
  My mind, still flying, turned me to survey
The track no living man e'er passed before.
Then, after easing my worn limbs with rest,
  On through that wilderness I wandered, still
  Keeping my lower foot most firmly prest;
When, lo! beginning now to climb the hill,    24
A leopard, glistening in a dappled hide,
  That would not fly, though light and full of speed,
Hindering my way, before me I descried,
  And often turned, as doubtful to proceed.

The time was morning; and the sun above
  The world was riding with his kindred stars,
  His old companions from the day when Love
Divine first moved those beautiful bright cars:    32
Hope cheered my heart to mark the dawning bright,
  The season sweet, the creature's lively dress;
  But soon a lion met my startled sight,
Whose fearful shape renewed my late distress.
With towering head he stalked and ravenous mien,
  Striding towards me, and seemed to shake the air:
  Next, came a she-wolf, — one that long hath been
The curse of millions dwelling in despair.    40

Meagre, but looking crammed with every lust,
  She caused such horror though my soul to creep,
  That I began to falter, and mistrust
  My power to win the summit of the steep.
I felt like one who, gladly gathering gain,
  Until some luckless time that brings him loss,
  Then, all disheartened, sorely doth complain —
  To see that restless beast my pathway cross. 48
With every stride she drove me slowly back
  Down where no Sun the stillness did illume;
  But while I thus was falling from my track,
  A form before me glimmered through the gloom,
Whom faintly marking, as obscure he seemed
  In the long silence of that desert glade,
  " Whate'er thou art, oh pity me!" I screamed —
  " Whether a living man, or but a shade." 56


" No man," he answered — " once I was a man;
  Mantua my Lombard parents called their home;
  In Julius' reign (though late) my life began,
  And, under good Augustus, passed at Rome.
In those false days, by lying gods o'errun,
  A Poet I, and sang of him who came
  From blazing Troy, Anchises' righteous son,
  When all proud Ilion melted in one flame. 64

But thou — so rough a struggle why repeat?
  Why rather climb not this glad mountain-side,
  Of all delight the source and happy seat?"
  Whereto, with bashful forehead, I replied:

" Art thou that VIRGIL then, the mighty spring
  Who pour'st of language that majestic stream?
  O light and glory of the race who sing!
  Let it avail me that, with love extreme
And zeal unwearied, I have searched thy book:
  Thou my choice author art, my Master thou,
  Thou the sole fountain whence my genius took
  The style whose grace gives laurel to my brow.
Behold yon monster in my road! whose rage
  Thrills through my veins until my pulses quake;
  Defend me from her, thou illustrious sage!"
  Whereat, observing how I wept, he spake:

" This savage wilderness if thou wouldst fly,
  For thee thy journey lies a different way;
  Since yonder brute, which wakes this piteous cry,
  Permits no mortal on her path to stray;
Nay, every trespasser with death prevents:
  So bad by nature, so accursed at core,
  Her greedy appetite she ne'er contents,
  But, after gorging, stills howls on for more.

With many a beast already she hath lain,
    And shall with many another, leagued in lust,
    Till come the Greyhound, slaying her with pain!
He will not feed on earthly dross and dust,
    But wisdom, love, and virtue: He shall dwell
    'Twixt the two Feltros: comfort He shall spread
O'er Latium's land, for which Camilla fell,
    Turnus, Euryalus, and Nisus bled. 96
'Tis He shall worry her through every town,
    Till back to Hell, wherefrom she first arose,
    Envy's rank spawn, He shall have dragged her down:
There, for thy good, to lead thee I propose.
Come, thou shalt follow me; and I will be
    Through regions infinite and dark thy guide,
    Where thou shalt hear the desperate shrieks, and see
Souls who for ages have in anguish cried, 104
'Oh for that second death!'—But happier some
    Shalt thou behold who dwell in flames content,
    Hoping at last amid the blest to come;
To whom wouldst thou hereafter make the ascent,
Unto a spirit worthier far than I,
    At parting, I must render thee; because
    He, the Great Potentate who reigns on high,
Found me rebellious to his holy laws. 112

He, through my guidance, therefore, none admits
   To His pure City. He reigns everywhere;
   But there His throne is, there He dwells and sits.
Happy, thrice happy whom He chooses there!"

Then I to him: "O Poet! I implore,
   Even by that God unknown to thee of old,
   So may I shun this misery and more,
   (Whatever worse remaineth to be told)       120
That thou wilt bring me to the mentioned place,
   Where I may look upon Saint Peter's gate,
   First having viewed the woes of that sad race."
Then He moved on, and I behind him straight.

## CANTO THE SECOND.

Day was departing, and the dusky light
Freed earthly creatures from their labor's load:
I alone girt me to sustain the fight, —
A strife no less with pity than my road,
Which memory now shall paint in truth's own hue:
O Muse! O soaring genius, help me here!
O mind, recording all that met my view!
Here must thy native nobleness appear.

DANTE.

Thus I began: " Oh thou who art my guide,
Poet! what strength my humble virtue hath
Examine well before, with steps untried,
My feet be trusted to that arduous path.
Thou tell'st of Silvius, how his Father went
Among the immortals, animated still
With sense, in flesh corruptible still pent, —
Such was His grace who hateth every ill;

But gracious Heaven weighed then the high result, —
   Both Who and What should spring from such a seed!
   Nor to man's reason seems the cause occult,
   Since He was in the empyreal sphere decreed
The future Father of benignant Rome,
   And of Rome's empire, which were pre-ordained
   To be the holy seat and sacred home
   Of him who sits where greater Peter reigned.
That visit, famed by thee o'er all the globe,
   Taught him the events wherefrom, in process grew
   His conquest, and, in fine, the Papal robe.
God's 'chosen vessel' journeyed heavenward too,
   To strengthen more that Faith wherein alone
   The primal steps of our salvation lie;
   But why to me were such indulgence shown?
   For no Æneas, no Saint Paul, am I;
Small is my worth in mine as men's esteem:
   Should I, so humble, so forlorn and weak,
   Venture this going, 'twould but folly seem:
   Thou'rt wise — more wise to hear than I to speak."

As one who wavers in his wish, — by doubt
   Discouraged wholly from his first design,
   Thus I, on Hell's dim coast, in thought wore out
   That eager spirit which before was mine.

## CANTO II.

#### VIRGIL.

"If I thy language rightly have conceived,"
Serenely answered that majestic shade,
"Thy mind of manhood is through fear bereaved,
Which oft a mortal bosom will invade,
That man from noble action, like a beast
Starting at some false vision, is deterred;
From which poor cowardice be now released!
Mark wherefore I am come, what I have heard,     48
When first for thee compassion touched my breast;
With those I dwelt who in suspense remain;
A Lady called me, beautiful and blest,
Whom I besought her mandates to explain.
Brighter her eyes beamed than the ruling star!
And thus she spake, in accents mild and low,
And tones all music, as an angel's are:

#### BEATRICE.

"Know, gracious Mantuan, gentle spirit! know     56
Thou whose fame lives and shall, till motion end!
In the wild waste, opposed upon his track,
A friend of mine, — yet ah! not fortune's friend,
Trembling with terror, from his way turns back;

And much, I fear, by what in heaven I heard,
　That I to succor him have risen too late,
　So far from his true pathway he has erred.
　Then hie thee, Virgil, with thy phrase ornate, 64
And with what else his rescue may require,
　By helping him, give comfort unto me;
For I am Beatrice who thus desire,
　And come from where again I fain would be.
Love called me hither, and I speak from Love:
　Full oft thy praise I will enforce on high,
　When I shall stand before my Lord above."


### VIRGIL.

The virgin ceased, and thus responded I: 72
"O soul of goodness! which alone mankind
　Exalts above all beings of the sphere,
　Whose heavenly orbit is the most confined,
Lady! thy sweet commandment charms mine ear
So that, already were thy wish obeyed,
　To my desire such readiness were slow;
　But tell me, why, from that large kingdom strayed,
Thy longed-for home, thou venturest here below." 80

## BEATRICE.

"Deeply thou questionest: briefly, then," she said,
"I will inform thee why, without alarm,
I wander hither: nothing is to dread,
Except those things that work a brother's harm.
Such things alone are to be feared; and such
   Have I been fashioned by the grace of God,
   That me thy misery hath no power to touch,
No, nor the flames of this austere abode.       88
In heaven, one Gentle Mourner so laments
   The sore distress I send thee to relieve,
   That in his rigor Justice half relents;
From her did Lucia this command receive:
'Now needs thy faithful one thy service,—go!
   To thy sole care his fortune I confide.'
   Then Lucia, cruelty's most constant foe,
Came where I sat by ancient Rachel's side:       96
'Why, BEATRICE, true praise of God!' she said,
   'Dost thou not speed thee to befriend thine own,
   Who for thy love the vulgar crowd hath fled?
Hearest thou not the misery of his moan?
Seest thou the death wherewith he now must cope
   By that dark stream whose waves like ocean's toss?'
   Never did worldling fly so swift, in hope
Of making profit or in fear of loss       104

As I, thus hearing her mine office teach,
  Left my blest seat, and hither hastening came,
  Putting my trust in thy majestic speech,
  Which honors thee and gives thy pupils fame."

VIRGIL.

" After thus arguing, she turned away
  Those radiant eyes which piteous drops did fill:
  This gave me speed; and thus, without delay,
  I came to thee, obedient to her will. 112
'Twas I who saved thee from the She-Wolf's wrath,
  Which o'er that fair mount hindered so thy road;
  What now? What makes thee falter in thy path?
  Why should thy heart so timidly forbode?
Why art not fearless, resolute, and free,
  Since three such beings, beautiful and blest!
  Even in the courts of heaven, watch over thee,
  And so much good my promise hath exprest?" 120

As flowerets, by the frosty breath of night
  Shut up and drooping, soon as daylight glows,
  Spring on their stems all open and upright,
  Even so my wearied courage freshly rose;

CANTO II.   13

And such gay spirits coursed my bosom through,
  That now, enfranchised, I was bold to say,
  " Oh pitying soul to my relief that flew,
  And gracious thou so quickly to obey!     128
The truth alone that gentle angel spake
  In her kind words, and thou no less with thine
  Dost in my bosom such desire awake,
  That gladly I renew my first design.
Then, since one wish conducts us both, lead on!
  Thou art my lord, my master, and my guide."
  Thus I addressed the shadow, and anon
  Through the steep woody way began to glide.     136

## CANTO THE THIRD.

THROUGH ME YOU REACH THE CITY OF DESPAIR
THROUGH ME ETERNAL WRETCHEDNESS YE FIND
THROUGH ME AMONG PERDITION'S TRIBE YE FARE
JUSTICE INSPIRED MY LOFTY FOUNDER'S MIND
POWER LOVE AND WISDOM — HEAVENLY FIRST MOST HIGH
CREATED ME. BEFORE ME NOUGHT HAD BEEN
SAVE THINGS ETERNAL — AND ETERNE AM I
LEAVE HERE ALL HOPE O YE WHO ENTER IN.

These words upon a gateway, overhead,
In blackest letters written, I discerned.
"Master, their sense is terrible," I said;
And thus to me the ready sage returned:
"Perish each coward thought! be firm, be bold:
We've reached the place wherein, as told thou wast,
The miserable race thou shalt behold,
Who of the intellect all fruit have lost."

## CANTO III.

And thereupon my hand he took in his,
  With a glad look, fresh courage to bestow,
  And straight unfolded all the mysteries,
  'Mid sighs, laments, and hollow howls of woe,
Which, loud resounding through the starless air,
  Forced tears of pity from mine eyes at first;
  For divers tongues and horrid language there,
  With words of agony, wrath's frequent burst,    24
Shrieks, and hoarse outcries, with a noise of hands,
  Mingling for ever, vex, in tumult strange,
  As when a whirlwind tosses round the sands,
  That air whose tints come from no season's change.

And I, my head in stupid horror bound,
  Said, "Master, tell me, what is this I hear?
  What wretched souls are these in anguish drowned?"
  To which he answered, "This award severe    32
On those unhappy spirits is bestowed,
  Of whom nor infamy nor good was known,
  Joined with that wicked crew which, unto God
  Nor false nor faithful, served themselves alone.
Heaven drove them forth, Heaven's beauty not to stain;
  Nor will the deep Hell deign to have them there
  For any glory that the damned might gain."
"Master," I asked, "what torment must they bear?    40

Why of such suffering are such groans begot?"
"Briefly," said he, " to die they have no hope;
Envious they are of every other lot,
In such a blind and grovelling state they grope:
The world their hateful memory doth contemn;
Mercy herself would scorn for them to plead;
Justice disdains them — we'll not speak of them:
Give them a glance, one only, and proceed." 48

Then I, still gazing, saw a flag unfurled,
That seemed as angry at a moment's rest,
So swiftly, as 'twas borne along, it whirled;
And after it a countless legion pressed.
Such multitudes I ne'er could have believed
By conquering Death had ever low been laid;
And some I recognized — there I perceived
Him who through fear that Great Refusal made. 56
At once I understood their kind, and knew
That God himself, and those with God at strife,
Alike despised that execrable crew —
Dead souls, which, even when living, had no life.
Naked they were, and stung from toe to crown
By wasps and hornets buzzing round them thick.
From their scarred faces to their feet streamed down
Tears, mixed with blood, which loathsome worms did
lick. 64

Now, gazing farther still, I could discern
   A crowd upon a river's ample shore:
   "Who are those, master? what, I fain would learn,
   Makes them appear thus anxious to pass o'er?
Through the dim light such look methinks I trace —"
   "These things," he answered, "thou shalt know anon,
   Soon as we stay our footsteps for a space
   Beside the dismal strand of Acheron."     72
Then, fearing lest too freely I had spoke
   What to my guide importunate might seem,
   I bent mine eyes, abashed, nor silence broke,
   Until we reached the border of the stream.

And towards us, in a vessel, rowing, lo!
   An aged, hoary man, with hair snow-white,
   Came crying, "Woe to ye, bad spirits, woe!
   Never hope ye to enjoy Heaven's blessed sight.     80
I come to bear ye to the other bank;
   In darkness infinite, in heat, in cold.
   But thou, who still dost with the living rank,
   Begone! nor mingle with the dead so bold."
Then, seeing that obedience I declined:
   "Some other way approach the strand!" quoth he;
   "You pass not here — another ferry find:
   Some less o'erloaden bark must carry thee!"     88

"Vex not thyself, O Charon! thus 'tis willed,
  Where what is willed is done — demand no more:"
  My leader thus the shaggy helmsman stilled,
  Who pilots all that livid marish o'er.
Round his red eyes rolled wheels of living flame;
  But those tired ghosts, quivering like naked birds,
  Their teeth all chattering, paler still became,
  Soon as they caught the inexorable words.
Then God Almighty they blasphemed, and those
  From whom they sprung, their parents and their kin,
  The human race, the seed wherefrom they rose,
  The hour and place they were engendered in.

So, as all must who fear not God, the shoal
  Withdrew, loud howling, toward that sinful shore;
  Fiend Charon, with his eyes of burning coal,
  Beckoning them, beats each laggard with his oar,
And gathers them together as they drop,
  Like leaves in autumn, falling thickly round,
  Each after each, till every towering top
  Yields all its yellow vesture to the ground:
Even, in like manner, Adam's seed impure,
  Throw from the brink their figures, one by one,
  At given signs, as birds obey the lure,
  Then glide together o'er the waters dun.

And, ere they have departed, draweth nigh
  Another spectral army to the strand.
  " Son!" said my gracious master, " all who die
In their God's wrath meet here from every land.
Justice divine still goads them onward so
  That very fear becomes desire at last;
  And o'er the flood right willingly they go:
By·no good spirit ever is it passed.           120
Therefore did Charon of thyself complain;
  And what he meant thou comprehendest now."

He ceased — the gloomy region shook amain!
  Still its mere memory bathes with sweat my brow.
Rumbled that land of tears with moaning wind:
  A light, vermilion-colored, flashed from Hell,
  And wholly vanquishing my palsied mind,
Even as a man whom sleep o'ertakes, I fell.     123

## CANTO THE FOURTH.

My brain's deep sleep was broken by a stroke
  Of jarring thunder, so that roused upright,
  Like one by sudden violence awoke,
  With eyes refreshed, I rolled around my sight;
And fixedly I gazed, the place to know
  Wherein I found me: o'er the brink I hung
  Of the dread valley of the abyss of woe,
  Whence gathered groans in ceaseless thunders rung.  8
Dark, fathomless it yawned; clouds o'er it curled:
  Down in its depths I pored, but nought discerned:
  "Descend we now to yonder rayless world,'
  The Poet said, and paler still he turned;
" But be thou second — I will go the first."
  To this I answered, noticing his hue,
  " If thou'rt dismayed who still my strength hast nurst?
  How shall I dare this journey to pursue?"  16

Then he to me: " The anguish that you hear
  Of those who moan below there makes my face
  Pallid with pity, deem not that I fear:
  But come, our long road chides this lingering pace."

Herewith he entered, and conveyed me in
  To the First Circle of the pit profound,
  Where nought distinct I heard, but one low din
  Of sighs that shook the eternal breeze around ;
Sighs born of mental, not of corporal throes,
  'Mid countless crowds of women, babes, and men.
  " Dost thou not ask," my good lord said, " who those
  Spirits are yonder, just within thy ken?
Ere thou go farther, to thy knowledge add,
  They did not sin : if so far they have meed,
  'Tis not enough, since they no baptism had ;
  This doctrine being portion of thy creed.
Christ's coming, too, since they were born before
  (And numbered with such hapless ones am I)
  They could but ignorantly God adore,
  For which deficiency alone we die ;
Punished thus far, that in desire we dwell,
  Ceaseless desire where hope hath never birth."
  I grieved to hear him, for I knew right well
  Hung in that Limbo many a soul of worth.

"Tell me, my master, tell me, Sire," I said,
   (To assure that Faith which sets all doubt at rest)
   " By his own merits, or another's sped,
   Went any ever hence to join the Blest?"
Then he, who well my inmost meaning knew,
   Answered: " Herein I had not long been bound,
   When an All-puissant One I saw march through,
With victory's radiant sign triumphal crowned.
He led from us our Father Adam's shade;
   Abel, and Noah whom God loved the most;
   Lawgiving Moses, who that law obeyed;
   Abra'am the patriarch; royal David's ghost;
Israel, his Father and his sons; and her
   Whom Israel served for faithfully and long,
   Rachel, with more, to bliss did he transfer:
No souls were saved before this chosen throng."

During these words our pace we did not slack,
   But passed the forest — forest let me say —
   So thickly swarmed the spirits round our track.
   Nor had we far descended on our way,
When, through the gloom of that black hemisphere,
   A light I noticed which the darkness quelled,
   And partly saw, though still not very near,
   A race of dignity that region held.

"Thou who all knowledge honor'st, and all art!
  What souls are those who seem thus glorified,
  That from the others they are set apart?"
  "Their names," he said, "are sounded far and wide;
Some grace Heaven grants them, for thy world's esteem."
  So speaking, fell a voice upon mine ear,
  "Honor and glory to the Bard Supreme!
  Whose shade which left us lately now draws near."
Then, as this voice grew quiet, and was hushed,
  Four mighty shades I saw advancing, dim,
  No sorrow paled their cheeks nor gladness flushed;
  "Look!" my good Master said, "take note of Him,
The first, who bears a sword, and chief is reckoned —
  'Tis HOMER, of all bards the sovereign classed;
  HORACE the satirist, he comes the second;
  The third is OVID; LUCAN is the last;
Since all their voices, mingling thus in one,
  Give me a title which alike we share,
  They do me honor, and 'tis nobly done."
  Thus the whole school I saw assembled, fair,
Of Him, song's loftiest lord, that o'er the rest
  Soars like an eagle: they conferred awhile,
  Then, me saluting, much good-will exprest,
  Whereat my Master blandly deigned to smile.

Nay, honor they devised for me still higher,
  In bidding me with their sage throng unite,
  So I was sixth amid that learned choir,
  And on we moved, still travelling toward the light.
Speaking of things best unsaid, in my rhymes,
  Though there becoming, we pursued our road
  Toward a proud castle, walled about seven times;
  Round which, a fair defence, a streamlet flowed. 96
O'er this we passed, as it had solid been,
  And through seven gates, with our companions wise,
  Entered a meadow fresh with living green,
  Where dwelt a race with grave, majestic eyes.
Authority was writ in every face;
  Sweetly they spake — but seldom: we withdrew
  Into an open, luminous high place,
  So that the whole were facile to my view. 104

Straight was I shown, on that enamelled mead,
  Those mighty spirits whom the world commends —
  Whom to have looked on, makes me proud indeed:
  I saw Electra circled with her friends;
Hector I marked; Æneas mid the ring;
  Cæsar, all armed, and, like a hawk, fierce-eyed;
  Penthesilèa, with Camilla; king
  Latinus resting by Lavinia's side. 112

## CANTO IV.

Brutus I saw, who Tarquin's tribe expelled;
   Cornelia, Marcia, Julia, chaste Lucrece —
   And Saladin sequestered I beheld:
   Then, looking up, that master sage of Greece,
The Stagirite, who sat all-honored there
   Girt with his philosophic household band:
   Plato I saw and Socrates, — this pair,
   Before their fellows, next the leader stand.    120
Thales I saw, and Zeno at a glance,
   With Anaxagoras; Diogenes;
   Democritus, who lays the world to chance;
   Heraclitus; Orpheus; Dioscorides,
Good herbalist that was; Empedocles;
   Seneca; Livy; Tully — matchless men!
   Earth-measuring Euclid; Ptolemy; by these
   Galen, Hippocrates, and Avicen:    128
Averroës, that commentator vast —
   But ah! of all I cannot duly speak,
   My long theme presses and, — my power surpassed,
   Oft, what I tell compared with truth is weak.

Our company of six in twain divide:
   Now from the tranquil to the trembling air
   Leads me, another way, my sapient guide
   Where no more light is — darkness everywhere.    136

## CANTO THE FIFTH.

From that First Circle parting thus, I went
  Down to the next, which girds a lesser space,
  And so much worse dole, stinging to lament:
  There Minos grinning stands with hideous face:
He scans the offences of each comer-in:
  When the bad soul its guilt hath fully told,
  He knows its place, and judgeth every sin,
  As in strange wise his form he doth infold:      8
How many grades, according to their crimes,
  Each must descend, he noteth by his tail,
  Winding it round his loins so many times;
  Numbers before him always wait and wail.
By turns they come to judgment and confess,
  And hear their doom, then down are hurried straight.
  "O thou, who seek'st this mansion of distress,"
  Cried Minos, pausing in his work of fate,      16

## CANTO V.

"Beware! beware in whom thou wouldst confide;
   Take heed of entering — trust not this broad way!"
"Wherefore this empty clamor?" said my guide:
   "His destined passage dare not thou to stay!
Vex thee not, Minos, even thus 'tis willed
   Where what is willed is done — demand no more!"
Now are mine ears with notes of anguish thrilled;
   Now new moans pierce me, numberless and sore.   24

I reached a spot with scarce a glimmer blest,
   Which roared like ocean torn by warring storms:
The infernal blast, which never knoweth rest,
   In furious wreck whirls on the shadowy forms,
Driving and madly dashing them along;
   And, when, as 'twere, destruction's brink they reach,
Then shriek, and scream, then yell the frantic throng,
   Yea, heaven's High King blaspheme with horrid speech.   32
Such pangs, I found, those unchaste sinners feel
   Who to low impulses the reason bowed;
And like as starlings, in the winter, wheel
   Their airy flight, — a large, wide-wavering crowd,
So that fierce gust these erring spirits blows
   This way and that way, up and down the cope;
Nor can they find, I say not of repose,
   But of diminished pain, one moment's hope.   40

Or like as cranes, a melancholy swarm,
   Go moaning through the air, in one long trail,
   So I beheld, before the pelting storm,
   Those ghosts fast flying with incessant wail.

"Master," I asked, "what multitude is that,
   Scourged 'mid this murky air to such extreme?"
   "The foremost of them," he replied, "once sat
   Empress o'er many-languaged lands Supreme.    48
In lust she grew so boundless and so free,
   That (haply so to vindicate her shame)
   She rendered lewdness lawful by decree;
   Semiramis that is, well known to fame.
The land the Sultan sways she ruled in pride,
   To Ninus the successor and the spouse:
   The other is the amorous suicide,
   Who to Sicheus' ashes brake her vows."    56
Voluptuous Cleopatra next I saw;
   Helen, through whom such years of woe were passed!
   On great Achilles next I looked with awe,
   Who fought with love eternal to the last.
Paris and Tristan then, and many more,
   More than a thousand shadows as they flew,
   He pointed out to me, and named them o'er,
   On earth whom Love's unhallowed passion slew.    64

When I had heard my teacher call by name
  These knights and ladies of the olden time,
  My wildered soul compassion quite o'ercame,
  And I began: " Great builder of the rhyme!
Fain would I speak with yonder pair who glide
  Together, light before this whirlwind borne."
  " Watch them till they draw nearer," he replied;
  " Then, by that love which leads them here to mourn,
Beseech them, — they will come." Whereat I did
  Invoke them, when the gale had blown them near:
  " O troubled spirits! come, unless forbid
  By some High Power, your story let us hear!"

As wandering doves, bound homeward through the sky,
  Called by desire, with wings wide open thrown,
  Steadily toward their pleasant dwellings fly,
  Sped ever onward by their wish alone;
So, from the troop where Dido ranks, they sailed
  Toward me, through that dim atmosphere malign,
  My passionate entreaty so prevailed:

" O breathing being, gracious and benign!
Who com'st to visit through this crimson air
  Us, whose heart's blood hath stained the world above,
  To Him who rules the universe, our prayer
  Should rise for thy soul's peace, — had we His love;

And, since thou pitiest thus our ill-starred fate,
   Listen, — or speak; for, whatsoe'er ye will,
   We will as freely hear of as relate,
While this dread blast is, for the moment, still.

"My native city stands upon the shore
   Where Po descends in Adria's peace to rest,
   Raging with all his rivulets no more.
   Love, quick to kindle every gentler breast,      96
Fired this fond being with the lovely shape
   Bereft me so! — I shudder at the way:
   Love, who permits no loved one to escape,
   That I pleased him, charmed me with equal sway;
Even here thou seest the rapture hath not died;
   And Love led both of us to one fell death:
   But Cain's own pangs our murderer must bide."
These were the words borne to me by their breath.   104

Listening these injured souls, I hung my head
   So low, — "What think'st thou?" said the bard. "Alas!
   What tender thoughts, how strong desire," I said,
   "Brought those two lovers to their woful pass!"
Then, turning round to them, I thus began:
   "Francesca! tears must overflow mine eyes,
   My pitying soul thy martyr-throes unman;
   But tell me, — in the time of happy sighs,     112

Your vague desires how gave Love utterance first?"
And she to me: "The mightiest of all woes
Is, in the midst of misery, to be cursed
With bliss remembered — this thy teacher knows.
Yet, wouldst thou learn our passion's root and head,
As one may speak whose eyes with tears are dim,
So will I speak. Together once we read
The tale of Lancilot — how love seized him. 120
Alone we were, without suspecting aught:
Oft in perusal paled our cheeks their hue,
And oft our eyes each other's glances caught;
But one sole passage 'twas which both o'erthrew.
At reading of the longed-for smile, — to be
By such a lover's kissing so much blest,
This dearest, — never shalt thou part from me!
His lips to mine, to mine, all trembling, pressed. 128
The writer was our Galeot with his book:
That day we read no farther on." She stopped:
Meanwhile he moaned so that compassion took
My sense away, and like a corse I dropped.

## CANTO THE SIXTH.

My mind returning, which had been so drowned
In pity, listening to that kindred pair,
Wildered with grief, I mark, on gazing round,
New pangs, new victims writhing everywhere.
Where'er I move, where'er mine eye explores
The peopled gloom, where'er I turn again;
For the Third Circle now I reach, where pours
One heavy, cursed, cold, relentless rain. 8
Thick, muddy water, snow and hailstones coarse
That rayless atmosphere, eternal, drench;
Ceaseless the flood, unchanged in kind or force:
The land it soaks is putrid with one stench.
Fell monster Cerberus with hideous clack
Barks at the sinners from his triple jaws;
Red eyes he hath; a beard bedaubed and black;
A stomach turgid; armed with fangs his paws. 16
'Tis his the unholy crew to tear and rend
Whose yells are like the howlings of a hound
In that mad storm; and often, to defend
One with the other side, they turn them round.

CANTO VI.

When Cerberus, that serpent's offspring grim,
  Spied us, his mouths he opened, and exposed
  His jaggy tusks, quivering in every limb.
Hereat my guide stooped down, with hands unclosed,   24
And filled them with a portion of the mire
  Which down those ravenous throats he straightway cast.
  As bays a greedy dog with fierce desire,
But quiet grows, mumbling the snatched repast
For which alone his hunger fights and strains;
  Even so were hushed those ugly gullets three
  Of devilish Cerberus, whose howl so pains
The dizzy ghosts that deaf they long to be.   32

We walked o'er shadows by the bitter sleet
  Battered and crushed; and on their empty forms,
  Which seemed corporeal, trod with trembling feet,
  As on the ground they lay in huddling swarms.
All saving one, which started up and said,
  As on we strode past that poor, sitting ghost,
  " O thou who through this horrid Hell art led!
. Speak,—recognize me, if my face thou know'st;   40
Before I died, full surely thou wast born."
  " Haply," said I, " thy tortures here erase
  All recollection of that look forlorn:
Till now, methinks I never saw thy face.

Tell, then, who art thou, in this region dun,
   Shut up 'mid such foul agonies to pine?
   Greater there may be — more disgusting, none."
   Said he, " Thy native city once was mine:        48
Within those walls, which with an envious crew,
   Like a heaped sack, run o'er, my sweet life passed.
   Ciacco, my townsmen! I was called by you:
   Through Gluttony's damned sin I fell at last.
Thence am I thus by this fierce tempest bruised;
   No single sufferer: all this wretched herd,
   My brother-ghosts, are thus severely used
   For a like fault." He ended with this word.        56

" Ciacco," said I, " thy miserable fate
   Tempts me to tears, and weighs my manhood down;
   But tell me, if thou know'st, what griefs await
   The citizens of that divided town.
Dwells any just one there? — Inform me why
   'Tis thus o'erwhelmed in discord's raging flood?"
   " After long contests," this was his reply,
   " The opposing sides shall come at last to blood.     64
The rustic faction shall in fury drive
   The other out, but soon itself must bow:
   Within three suns, that other shall revive,
   Strong in his aid who comes, a neutral, now.

Long time a lofty port it shall sustain,
  Making its foes beneath harsh burdens groan,
  Howe'er they chafe and fret themselves in vain:
  Just persons two there are — unheard, unknown.   72
  Envy and Pride and Avarice — these three
  Pernicious sparks have set all hearts on fire."
  He ended, speaking in this mournful key.
" Say on!" I cried; " grant further my desire.
Tegghiaio, Farinata, both confessed
  Such worthy men, — Arrigo, Mosca too,
  Jacopo Rusticucci, with the rest
  Who bent their talents virtuous deeds to do, —   80
Fain would I greet them: tell me if they dwell
  (An earnest longing thrills my soul to know)
  Soothed by Heaven's airs, or poisoned in this Hell?"
Said he, " With blacker souls they're sunk below;
For different faults down towards the bottom hurled:
  If thou descend, their spirits thou mayst see.
  Oh! when once more thou walk'st the pleasant world,
  Then I implore thee to remember me!   88
I say no more, nor farther give reply."
  He hung his head, and turned his face away;
  Scanned me a little with a sidelong eye;
  Fell 'mid those groping ghosts, and grovelling lay.

Here spake my guide: "Nothing shall rouse him now,
   Till, when the angelic trump shall rend earth's womb,
   Their Mighty Foe shall come with radiant brow:
Then each again must find his dismal tomb;    96
Then each his flesh and figure shall regain,
   To hear the pealing of the eternal doom."
So with slow footsteps, 'mid the noisome rain,
   Mixed up with shades, we struggled through the gloom.

And touching slightly on the future state,
   "Master," said I, "the pangs which these abide,
   After the Judgment, will they be as great,
Or less, or worse?"—"Return thee," he replied,    104
   "To thy philosophy, which teaches this:
   As grows a thing more perfect, even so
Its sense grows keener, both of pain and bliss.
Ne'er can these wretches true perfection know;
   Yet must they look to be more perfect then."
With this, and more which I forbear, we wound
   About that road until it sloped again:
Here Plutus, that arch-enemy, we found.    112

## CANTO THE SEVENTH.

Ho! Satan! Popes — more Popes — head Satan! here!
  Plutus began with accent harsh and hoarse;
  Whereat the omniscient sage, my soul to cheer,
  Said, " Fear not thou, nor falter in thy course:
Thy destined passage down this craggy path
  He shall not hinder; vain is all his might."
  Then turning to those lips that swelled with wrath,
  " Silence, curst wolf!" he cried; " keep down thy
On thine own entrails let thy fury feed.      [spite;
  Not without warrant are these depths explored:
  'Tis willed on high, where Heaven's adulterous breed,
  Proud rebels! fell by Michael's vengeful sword."
As well-filled sails which in the tempest swell,
  Drop, with folds flapping, if the mast be rent;
  So to the earth that cruel monster fell,
  And straightway down to Hell's Fourth Pit we went. 16

Now deeper yet we pierced that doleful coast,
  Earth's universal evil which contains:
  Justice of God! who heapest such a host
As there I witnessed of new throes and pains,
Why of our crime such scourges do we make?
  Since not the leaping waves which upward spout
  O'er wild Charybdis, when they clash and break,
Than this damned crew, more madly whirl about.   24

For here I marked a still more numerous flock,
  With shrieks and tugging breasts, from side to side
  Rolling huge weights, which struck with violent shock:
Then, turning round, they rolled them back, and cried,
In mutual censure, "Why so close to keep?"
  And "Why so eager ye to throw away?"
  Then, toward the point opposed, I saw them sweep,
On either hand, to meet in fresh affray.   32
Thus chanting ever their reproachful song,
  Thereby upbraiding still each other's fault,
  Back through their dismal round, the toiling throng
Like tilters came, renewing the assault.

Heart-stung with grief, I said: "O master mine!
What race is this? and those on our left hand,
With shaven crown, — the sacerdotal sign,
Belonged they to the clergy's holy band?"       40
"All these," he answered, "had their mental sight
So far distorted in life's former scene,
They never used their worldly wealth aright;
And this is plainly what these outcries mean,
As, doomed for different sins towards either bourn
Of this sad round, they diversely advance.
There, mid yon clergy, with their tresses shorn,
Popes lead with Cardinals the eternal dance:    48
Avarice o'er these once held sole masterdom."
"Teacher," said I, "amid that restless herd,
Surely acquainted I should be with some,
Who to my knowledge once so foully erred."
"Vain thought!" he answered; "since the dark disgrace
Of their ill-spent and ignominious life
Their forms from all remembrance doth efface.
Here aye they clash in this perpetual strife:    56
Those with clipped locks, and these with fists shut close,
Shall quit their sepulchres — for all were thrust
Either by Avarice or Profusion gross
From the fair world to encounter in this joust.

I will not smooth it o'er with phrases bland,
    Now mayst behold, my son, how brief a bubble
    Are those possessions, placed in Fortune's hand,
    For which thy race fret out their hearts with trouble;  64
Since all the gold that underneath the moon
    Was ever dug, or in the mine yet glows,
    Could not procure one weary soul the boon,
    The blessed pittance of an hour's repose.

" O master mine! still more I would be told:
    This Fortune whom thou mention'st,—what is she,
    Who seems all riches in her clutch to hold?"
" Poor creatures!" he exclaimed, " how blind are ye!  72
Through what excess of ignorance ye fall!
    Would ye might learn, from this discourse of ours,
    That He whose wisdom, so transcending all!
    Gave to the heavens he framed presiding powers,
That sphere to sphere might each responsive shine,
    And every part with equal radiance beam;
    So to earth's glories also did assign
    One general guide and guardian power supreme!  80
She in due turn wealth's empty dower translates
    From race to race, from blood to blood, unchecked;
    Hence come the glory and decay of states;
    Obeying all a power whom none suspect;

For like a serpent in the grass concealed,
  While mortal wisdom 'gainst her fights in vain,
  She, even as other gods their sceptres wield,
  Disposes, guides, and regulates her reign. 88
No truce to her mutations is allowed;
  Necessity compels her to move fast,
  So thick the claimants on her bounty crowd;
  She 'tis at whom such mangling terms are cast:
Even those who most should praise, blaspheme her most;
  But her their curses little can annoy,
  For blest is she; and, with her fellow-host,
  The first created, fills her sphere in joy. 96
Now to more piteous torments we'll descend,
  Since every star which showed its rising ray,
  When first I sped thy journey to befriend,
  Is sinking fast, and chides our long delay."


The Circle traversing, its brink we gained,
  Just o'er a filthy fount of purplish hue;
  This, boiling over, by a ditch was drained
  Which the dark water hardly struggled through. 104
Entering another way with that sad rill
  Whose inky dribblings down beside us crept,
  We still accompanied its course, until
  In that morass whose name is Styx they slept.

Here, at the scowling precipice's base,
    I stopped, intently gazing, and beheld,
    Plunged in that bog, a smeared but naked race,
    With wrathful eyes, and features passion-swelled.   112
These not with hands alone each other beat,
    But headlong rushed, butting and striking sore,
    Met breast to breast, and fought with furious feet,
    Yea, piecemeal with their teeth each other tore.

"Behold! my son," my gentle master said,
    "The souls of those whom Anger overthrew;
    And oh! believe me, in the loathsome bed
    Of this rank fen are myriads hid from view.   120
They sigh below, and by their sighing stir
    The surface bubbling, as you see, around.
    Fixed in the slime they murmur: 'Sad we were
    In the glad air, and on the sunshine frowned;
Still in our veins a sullen vapor floats,
    Sad in this dreggy bottom we remain.'
    This wretched psalm they gurgle in their throats,
    Too choked with mire distinctly to complain."   128

Thus, a great circuit making 'twixt the mud
    And the dry bank, we re-assumed our pace,
    Gazing on those who swilled the nauseous flood:
    At length we stopped beside a turret's base.

## CANTO THE EIGHTH.

RESUMING my suspended strain, I say,
  Ere to the foot of that high tower we came,
  Up roved our eyes, its summit to survey,
  Caught by a signal from a double flame.
Afar, another answering beacon burned
  Dimly and distant — almost out of sight.
  Unto that Sea of knowledge then I turned,
  And questioned him, " What means this lofty light ?    8
And who may those who fire yon cresset be ?
  " Yonder," said VIRGIL, " on the slimy bog,
  What is about to happen thou shalt see,
  Unless the fen conceal it with its fog."

Never an arrow bounded from a string,
  Whizzing so lightly through the upper air,
  As I beheld a bark, — a little thing,
  Cleave the thick, clouded flood, and toward us bear.    16

A single pilot steered it o'er the wave,
 Who cried — " Art come, dark spirit and abhorred ? "
 " Phlegyas ! Phlegyas ! vainly dost thou rave ;
 Bootless, this time, thy clamor," said my lord ;
" We are thine only while thou row'st across."
 Like one who inly grumbleth, when he hears
 Of some foul fraud whereby he suffereth loss,
 Grim Phlegyas in his gathering rage appears.  24
Then with my guide I stepped aboard the bark,
 Which, till my entering, seemed devoid of weight:
 Soon as I trod that vessel old and dark,
 The prow cut deeper with the unwonted freight.

As thus we ploughed through that dead sea of slime,
 One rose before me, all besmirched with clay,
 Growling, " Who'rt thou, who com'st before thy time ? "
 " To come," I answered him, " is not to stay.  32
But who art thou, so hideous in thy pain ? "
 " You see," he muttered, " I am one who mourn."
 " Curst spirit ! " I answered, " in thy pangs remain, —
 I know thee, even thus filthy and forlorn."
'Gainst us, both hands he lifted, with a frown ;
 Wary of which, the Master thrust him back,
 Crying, " Detested dog ! down with thee ! down !
 Go, beastly wretch, and join thy fellow-pack.  40

Then roundabout my neck his arms he threw,
  And kissed me, saying, "Thou indignant soul!
  Blessed! within whose womb thy burden grew:
  On earth, his arrogance brooked no control;
No gleam of goodness to his memory clings;
  Thence raves he thus for ever, mad with wrath:
  And oh! what numbers now are mighty kings,
  Who here, like swine, must wallow in this bath! 48
What execration shall their memories wake!"
  "Master," said I, "my wish 'twould mainly please,
  Before we disembark from this black lake,
  To see him, weltering, plunged beneath its lees."

He thus rejoined: "Before we come much nigher
  To yonder shore, which is not yet in sight,
  Thou shalt enjoy the full of thy desire,
  And witness what will give thy soul delight." 56
So, shortly, I beheld that loathsome race
  On the foul ghost with horrid fury fall;
  For which, my thanks I render to God's grace.
  "Philip Argenti! at him! each and all!"
This was their cry: the frantic Florentine
  With his own teeth his limbs in anguish tore,
  Helplessly raging 'gainst his foes obscene:
  We left the miscreant here — of him no more. 64

Now lamentations loud my hearing stun;
  Forward I send mine unimpeded eye,
  While thus my gracious master: "Now, my son,
We to the city, named of Dis, draw nigh.
There the sad residents by myriads grieve."
  "O master mine! its minarets and spires
  Plain from yon valley, peering I perceive,
  Vermilioned o'er, as rising out of fires."  72
"As thou descriest," he answered, "they are dyed
  By inward fires, in this low Hell unquenched."
So up the ditches we began to glide,
  Which that disconsolate domain intrenched.

The dismal town meseemed was iron-walled:
  A great way round we struggled through the scum,
  Until arrived where loud the helmsman bawled,
  "Out with ye! to the entrance ye are come."  80
Then I beheld toward those dark portals drive
  More than a thousand, hurled from heaven, who said
  In angry tones, "Who's this that still alive
Invades the gloomy kingdom of the dead?"
Here my sage master those proud spirits becked,
  That privately with them he fain would talk:
  Whereat, their contumely slightly checked,
  They said, "Walk hither then, but singly walk.  88

Let him so rashly venturing to this reign
    By his own wit retrace his foolish road:
    Ay let him try,—thou only shalt remain
    Who guard'st him through this terrible abode."
Think, reader, how I shuddered, as I heard
    The surly speech of that accursed crew;
    Foreboding sadly from each bitter word,
    That never more the sunlight I should view.    96
" O my dear guide! whose kindly hand," I said,
    " Through perils infinite and foes unknown,
    More than seven times my faltering feet has led,
    Leave me not now all helpless and alone!
Since further progress is to us denied,
    Together quickly let us travel back."
    Whereat my leader and my lord replied:
    " Fear not: our destined course no power can slack.    104
'Tis not for them to stop what Heaven ordains;
    Abide thou here, while I to greet them go;
    Cheer up! let hope invigorate thy veins,
    I'll not desert thee in this world below."

The gentle father leaves me here behind,
    To speak with them, while I remain in doubt,
    With no and yes contending in my mind;
    Nor could I hear what they conferred about:    112

But with our foes he did not long debate;
   For they, their swiftness putting to the proof,
   Rushed back, and bolted in his face the gate:
   Returned he then to where I stood aloof.
Slowly, with fitful pace and drooping lids
   And brow deject, he came, and sighing spake:
   " Who to yon dreary walls my way forbids?"
Then unto me: " What though mine ire they wake?   120
Fear not but in this contest I shall win,
   Let them against me struggle ne'er so hard:
   This gang ere now as insolent hath been
   Up at that portal found for aye unbarred.
Its fatal, dark inscription thou hast read;
   And even now, descending by the slope,
   Comes, without escort, through the Circles dread,
   ONE whose proud hand this region's gate shall ope."   128

## CANTO THE NINTH.

THE craven color which my face had shown,
  When sadly back I saw my leader glide,
  Soon checked the transient flushing of his own;
Hearkening he stood, intent and eager-eyed.
But ill his gaze could fathom that thick air
  As thus he spake: " In this approaching fray
  Conquer we must, — unless — but why despair?
Such help will come — O wearisome delay!"   8

I noted well how his conclusion veiled
  The doubtful words wherewith his speech began,
  So that the tenor of the sentence failed;
And through my heart a timid tremor ran,
For haply to his halting phrase I gave
  A worse construction than the poet meant.
  " Say, — to this depth of misery's concave
From the first round makes any soul descent   16

Of them whose only pain is hope's suspense?"
  To this inquiry thus my lord replied:
  " Rarely doth one of us, repricved from thence,
  Tread the dark way through which thy steps I guide.
Soon after I shook off my mortal part,
  'Tis true that hither once myself did stray,
  By fell Erictho conjured, — her whose art
  Could summon back dead spirits to their clay:
At her behest, I passed through yonder wall
  To lead one from the round where Judas dwells;
  The most removed from heaven, that circleth all —
  The deepest, darkest, worst of all the hells.
I know the road: thy vain mistrust forbear;
  The marsh o'er which these noisome vapors brood
  Girdles and guards the City of Despair,
  Where, without strife, none ever can intrude."

And more he said, which I remember not,
  Having been wholly ravished by mine eye,
  Toward the tower's top, which glistened crimson hot,
  While flashed in sight three hell-born fiends on high;
Furies, blood-stained, — female in limbs and air, —
  About their waists were greenest hydras wound;
  Horned snakes and vipers formed their horrid hair,
  Dangling in braids their savage temples round.

Then he who well the haggard handmaids knew
 Of everlasting sorrow's doleful queen,
 Exclaimed: "Look there! each fierce Erinnys view;
 Megæra yonder on thy left is seen;
There, on thy right, the sad Alecto wails;
 Betwixt them scowls Tisiphone." This spoke,
 He ceased. They tore their bosoms with their nails,
 Sore bruised themselves, and hideous outcries woke. 48
Close to the gentle bard I clung dismayed.
 "Bring forth Medusa! turn the wretch to stone!
 The assault of Theseus we too poorly paid:"
 Thus, glaring down, all shrieked with threatening tone.
"Turn!" cried the Poet—"cover quick thine eyes!
 Shouldst thou but glance upon the Gorgon's head,
 Never again couldst thou behold the skies."
 My hands distrusting, with his own instead, 56
He turned me round from their vindictive ire,
 And with his shadowy fingers veiled my gaze.
 O ye whose intellects are sound! admire
 The mystic meaning my strange verse conveys.

Swept now amain those turbid waters o'er
 A tumult of a dread, portentous kind,
 Which rocked with sudden spasms each trembling shore,
 Like the mad rushing of a rapid wind. 64

As when, made furious by opposing heats,
 Wild through the wood the unbridled tempest scours,
 Dusty and proud, the cringing forest beats,
 And scatters far the broken limbs and flowers;
Then fly the herds, — the swains to shelter scud.
 Freeing mine eyes, " Thy sight," he said, " direct
 O'er the long-standing scum of yonder flood,
 Where, most condense, its acrid streams collect."   72

As frogs before their enemy, the snake,
 Quick scattering through the pool in timid shoals,
 On the dank ooze a huddling cluster make,
 I saw above a thousand ruined souls
Flying from one who passed the Stygian bog,
 With feet unmoistened by the sludgy wave;
 Oft from his face his left hand brushed the fog
 Whose weight alone, it seemed, annoyance gave.   80
At once the messenger of Heaven I kenned,
 And toward my master turned, who made a sign
 That hushed I should remain and lowly bend.
 Ah me, how full he looked of scorn divine!

He reached the portals; with a little rod
 Touched them, — unbolted, instantly, they flew;
 Then, on the horrid threshold as he trod,
 " O heaven-expelled!" he 'gan, — " accursed crew!   88

What frantic pitch of insolence is this?
  Why vainly kick against the will Supreme,
  Whose mighty aim was never known to miss,
  Who to your pangs oft adds a new extreme?
Hope ye, in fighting with the Fates, to win?
  Your Cerberus,—bethink ye, to this day,
  Bears he not hairless his galled throat and chin?"
This said, he journeyed back his loathsome way.     96
Nor did he deign to notice us, but wore
  The look of one whom graver cares weigh down,
  Than any heed of whom he stands before:
  Securely then, advanced we toward the town.

His hallowed words fresh confidence inspired;
  The gates we passed without a farther fray;
  And I, who curiously to see desired
  Their state who pent in such a stronghold lay,     104
Soon as I entered, sent my gaze around,—
  And lo! a champain vast on every side,
  Where guilty torments reign and griefs abound,
  I mark with wonder, stretching far and wide.
Even as at Arles, where spreads the stagnant Rhone,
  Or hard by Pola, where Quarnaro's waves
  Bathe and bound Italy, the fields are strewn
  And rendered ridgy with a thousand graves,     112

So, though more horrible, this region seemed;
   For here 'mid sepulchres were sprinkled fires,
   Wherewith the enkindled tombs all-burning gleamed:
Iron more fiercely hot no art requires.
Their lids were all suspended,—from them rose
   Distressful groans and murmurings of lament,
   As though from wretches plunged in direst woes.
"Master," said I, "What sinners here lie pent?    120
What buried race thus mutter from the vaults?"
   He answered thus: "The Arch-Heretics behold!
   Leaders of sects, with all who shared their faults—
More than thou think'st these crowded caves infold:
Here like with like, each with his kind inurned,
   In tortures more or less intense are cast."
   So saying, to the right my master turned,
Then 'twixt the tombs and lofty towers we passed.    128

## CANTO THE TENTH.

Now by a narrow path my master winds,
  Conducting me 'twixt those tormenting tombs
  And the town walls. " O thou whose goodness finds
A passage for me through these impious glooms,
Speak, Sovran Wisdom! — satisfy my hope:
  May man behold the wretches buried here
  In these dire sepulchres? the lids are ope,
Each hangs upraised, — and none is watching near."    8

To this he answered, " When they come at last,
  Clothed in their now forsaken frames of clay,
  From dread Jehoshaphat, — the judgment past,
These flaming dens must all be barred for aye.
Here in their cemetery, on this side,
  With his whole sect is Epicurus pent,
  Who thought the spirit with its body died.
Soon, therefore, thy desire shall be content, —    16

Ay, and that wish which thou conceal'st from me:"
"Good guide," I said, "I only veil my heart,
    Lest of mine utterance I appear too free:
Thyself my monitor of silence art."

"O Tuscan! thou who com'st with gentle speech,
    Through Hell's hot city, breathing from the earth,
    Stop in this place one moment, I beseech:
Thy tongue betrays the country of thy birth.  24
Of that illustrious land I know thee sprung,
    Which in my day perchance I somewhat vexed."
    Forth from one vault these sudden accents rung,
So that I trembling stood with fear perplexed.
Then as I closer to my master drew,
    "Turn back! what dost thou?" he exclaimed in haste;
    "See! Farinata rises to thy view;
Now mayst behold him upward from his waist."  32

Full in his face already I was gazing,
    While his front lowered, and his proud bosom swelled,
    As though even there, amid his burial blazing,
The infernal realm in high disdain he held.
My leader then, with ready hands and bold,
    Forced me towards him, among the graves, to pace,
    Saying, "Thy thought in open words unfold."
So by his tomb I stood, beside its base.  40

Glancing upon me with a scornful air,
  "Who were thine ancestors?" he coldly asked.
Full free to answer, I would not forbear
My name or lineage, but the whole unmasked.
Slightly the spirit raised his haughty brows,
  And said, "Thy sires to mine were aye adverse,
To me, and to the cause I did espouse;
Wherefore their legions twice did I disperse."    48
"What though they banished were? they all returned,
  Each time of their expulsion," I replied;
"That is an art thy Party never learned."
Hereat arose a shadow at his side:

Uplifted on his knees he seemed to me,
  For his face only to his chin was bare;
And roundabout he stared, as though to see
If other mortal with myself were there.    56
But, when that momentary dream was o'er,
  Weeping he groaned, "If thou this dungeon dim,
Led by thy soaring genius, dost explore,
Where is my son? why bringest thou not him?"

"Not of myself I seek this realm forlorn:
  He who waits yonder marshals me my road;
Whom once, perchance, thy Guido had in scorn."
My recognition thus I fully showed;    64

For in the pangs on that poor sinner wreaked,
   And in his question, plain his name I read.
   Suddenly starting up, " What! what! " he shrieked,
   " Sayest thou, ' he had'? what mean ye! is he dead?
Doth heaven's dear light his eye no longer bless?"
   Perceiving how I hesitated then,
   Ere I responded to his wild address,
   Backward he sunk, nor looked he forth again.    72

But that proud soul who first compelled my stay
   The same unalterable aspect wore;
   Moved not his neck, nor turned him either way;
   Stood fixed; then thus continued as before —
" And if that art my brethren could not learn,
   It more torments me than this fiery couch;
   Yet, fifty times ere Hecate's visage burn,
   How hard that lesson is thyself shalt vouch.    80
But tell me, I implore thee, so mayst thou
   In the sweet world for evermore remain!
   Why that vindictive people still avow,
   In all their laws, their hatred of my strain?"

I thus: " The carnage and the vast defeat,
   Which dyed the waters of the Arbia red,
   Provoke such edicts from our Judgment-seat."
   Hereat the spirit sighed, and shook his head:    88

"Not singly," he replied, " in arms I rose,
   Nor without reason ; for the cause was just :
   But once I singly stood, when all her foes
   Would fain have laid my Florence in the dust ;
Then I, alone, opposed that base decree."
   " Prithee," said I, " this complicated knot
   Resolve, and set my tangled reason free,
   So be a long repose thy children's lot ! 96
If rightly I conceive you, it appears
   Your eyes foresee whatever Time's dark hand
   Is leading forward in the lapse of years,
   Yet of the present nought ye understand."

" True," he rejoined : " we see indeed, like those
   Whose vision is imperfect, things afar.
   Thus much of light the Lord of light bestows,—
   To all near objects wholly blind we are. 104
And nothing know we of your human state
   Save some one else our ignorance advise :
   So, when for aye is shut the Future's gate,
   Know, from that instant, all our knowledge dies."

Then, with repentance for my slowness wrung,
   " Tell," I entreated, " yonder fallen shade,
   His son still walks the breathing world among,
   And tell him why mine answer I delayed : 112

Say that my mind with misconceit was dim,
  Whereof thy teaching now has cleared my thought"—
  At this my Master called me back to him:
  Hastily then the spirit I besought;
" Say, with thyself what fellow-sufferers herd ? "
  " Upward," he answered, " of a thousand more,
  The second Frederic is here interred,
  The Cardinal too — the rest I'll not name o'er."    120

He vanished here and toward the ancient bard
  I paced, much pondering what the sentence meant,
  Which, as it seemed, foretold a doom so hard.
  He too moved onward, whispering as he went,
" Wherefore so pensive ? so bewildered why ?
  When the hid reason of my care I told,
  The sage thus counselled: " That dark prophecy,
  I charge thee, still in thy remembrance hold.    128
And mark thou this," — he raised his finger here,
  " When thou shalt stand before the gentle ray
  Of her to whose fair eye all things are clear,
  Thy life's whole pilgrimage will she display."
To the left hand my master turned him then:
  Quitting the wall, we toward the centre wound,
  By a small path, descending to a glen
  Whence a foul stench, uprising, floated round.    136

## CANTO THE ELEVENTH.

On the steep margin of a circling row
Of broken rocks, that formed a lofty bank,
We came above a crueller mass of woe,
In the deep gulf that steamed forth vapors rank.
To shun the foul excess, we drew behind
  A huge tomb's lid, whereon these words I read:
  " I hold Pope Anastasius here confined,
Whom from the ways of truth Photinus led."    8

" Slowly," said Virgil, " must we now descend,
That, somewhat first familiar grown thereby,
Our hardened sense these fumes may less offend."
" Yet let no time be therefore lost," said I:
" Some compensation find for this delay."
  " Mark, then, my son; for I thereof was thinking,
  Within these rocks," proceeded he to say,
" Three circles lie, in due gradation sinking,    16

Resembling those above, but less in size:
With condemned spirits crowded are they all;
That whoso mere sight hereafter may suffice,
Hear how and wherefore they are held in thrall.

The end of each bad act abhorred of Heaven
Is other's wrong, by violence or guile;
But, since mankind alone to fraud is given,
That sin is in esteem of God more vile. 24
Therefore the fraudulent are down more deep,
Suffering the penance of severer woes.
The violent the whole first circle keep,
Which three less rounds distinguish and compose;
For man by force three persons may offend:
Himself, his God, his neighbor, he may wrong,—
I mean, as clearly thou shalt comprehend,
Them, or whatever doth to them belong. 32
His neighbor's person he may violate
By deadly strokes, by agonizing wounds;
May waste or burn or plunder his estate:
Hence the first ring with homicides abounds.
Therein assassins, thieves and plunderers hive,
Tormented all, and classed in various bands.
Man, too, himself of being may deprive,
Or on his own goods lay destructive hands. 40

In the succeeding round all such repent,
  Who, in your world, their being dare destroy,
  Who see God's noble gifts ignobly spent,
  Yea, dwell in misery where they should enjoy.
Lastly, the Deity is wronged by them,
  Who, in the covert of their secret hearts,
  Blaspheme Him, or deny Him, or contemn
  Nature, and all the gifts her grace imparts.         48
Therefore the last division sets its seal
  On all that in their hearts gainsay God's laws:
  Cahors and Sodom shall its vengeance feel.

Now, as for fraud, which every conscience gnaws,
This wrong in twofold way a man may do,—
  On him who doth, or who doth not confide:
  The latter manner, it is plain, breaks through
  The bond of Love, which Nature's hand hath tied.    56
Hence the next circle hypocrites infest,
  Dealers in magic, and all bartering knaves;
  There simony and robbery have their nest;
  Panderers and flatterers — all such filthy slaves.
The other mode not only holds in scorn
  Love's native instinct, but the acquired good-will
  Whereof a special confidence is born.
Thence, in the least and lowest circle still,         64

Where, in the centre of the world, Dis reigns,
    Traitors in flame for evermore consume."
"Master," said I, " thy clearness well explains
This gulf, its people, and their various doom :
But say, — those wretches in the unctuous marsh ;
    Those whom the gale drives, — those the rains torment,
And those who clashing meet, with language harsh,
    Why not within the fiery city pent?     72
Why, — if the Almighty hold them in His wrath,
    If not, then wherefore in such pangs confined?"

" Whither," he answered, " from its wonted path
    Of reason, wanders thy distracted mind?
Hast thou the memorable words forgot,
    Wherein thy Ethic volume treats of three
    Ill-dispositions Heaven approveth not, —
Incontinence, malice, mad brutality?     80
And how incontinence doth less offend
    Almighty God, — less culpable by far?
If to this doctrine thou attention lend,
    Remembering who those other sinners are,
Those that above in late repentance pine,
    Thou shalt perceive why torments less severe
    Have been assigned them by the Judge divine,
And why they're separate from the wicked here."     88

## CANTO XI.

"O Sun! who purgest each beclouded sight,
 Thy clear solution satisfies me so,
 That doubt and knowledge equally delight;
 Yet back, I pray thee, for a little, go!
Thou said'st before, that usury offends
 Goodness divine: this knot now disengage."


"Philosophy," said he, "this lesson lends
 To him who searcheth, in full many a page,
That Nature ever in her course pursues
 The mode of action of the Sovereign Mind;
 And, if thy Physics rightly thou peruse,
 This truth, ere many pages, thou shalt find:
That, as a pupil in his master's course,
 Your Art strives after Nature, as it were
 Grandchild of God! — from whom it hath its source.
 By these, if thou to Genesis refer,
God said that man must live, and raise his race.
 Now, from this law the usurer doth depart,
 His best hope building upon something base:
 Therefore both Nature he contemns and Art.


But follow me, — my feet impatient are:
 Above the horizon's verge the Fishes leap;
 All o'er the Northwest spreads the glittering Car,
 And far our path declines down yonder steep."

## CANTO THE TWELFTH.

THE cliff we came to, where our passage lay,
  Was rough and Alpine, and an object bore
  Which every eye had shrunk from in dismay;
  For, like the fallen mass which struck the shore
Of trembling Adige, on this side of Trent,
  Ill-propped, or loosened by some earthquake, so
  That from the summit, whence the rock was rent,
  Some way is opened to the vale below,—
Such was the steep,— so pathless, and so rude;
  And o'er it, stretched upon the broken pile,
  There lay the adulterate heifer's loathsome brood,
  The shame, the monster of the Cretan isle.
He gnawed his limbs, observing us advance,
  Like one from inward rage that seeks relief,
  Whereat my sage conductor cried, "Perchance
  Thou deemest this to be the Athenian chief

Who shed thy life-blood in the world above.
  Brute thing, avaunt! — this visitant with me
  Comes not befriended by thy sister's love:
  He only comes your punishments to see."
As doth a bullock, plunging, when he feels
  The deadly stroke that brings him to the ground, —
  Who cannot go, but sidelong springs and reels,
  So did I see the Minotaur reel round.                24
" Run!" cried my wary lord, " while thus in wrath;
  Best thou make speed; betake thee to the strait."
  So down we clambered, and the rocky path
  Oft shook beneath my feet's unwonted weight.

Pensive I went; and my observant sage
  Addressed me thus: " Perchance thy thought is filled
  With this vast ruin, guarded by the rage
  Of the fell beast whose fury I have stilled.         32
Now learn, that when I travelled here of old,
  Down this way to the depths of lower Hell,
  This precipice was not, as you behold,
  Shattered and rent; but, if I rightly spell,
Just ere He came who bore the spoil from Dis,
  Of the First Circle, ransomed, up above,
  So shook throughout this deep and foul abyss,
  Methought the universe was seized with Love,        40

Which oft, as some believe, with violent shock
   Hath into chaos changed again the world;
   And here, and more elsewhere, this ancient rock,
   At that dread moment, was in fragments hurled.
But gaze down yonder: we approach the flood
   Where all, who violent 'gainst others were,
   Welter and writhe in waves of boiling blood."
O foolish wrath! blind passion! O thou spur
That goadest us through life's brief scene of being,
   And after plungest us in endless woe!
   A moat I saw, with my guide's words agreeing,
   Of ample width and bending like a bow:
While thus it seemed to compass all the plain,
   Between it and the precipice's base
   Ran Centaurs, armed with arrows, in a train;
   As, in the world, they once pursued the chase.

They stopped at seeing us advance; and three
   Rushed with their bows, their arrows choosing first;
   And one cried out afar off, "What seek ye?
   What destined round adown the cliff accursed?
Speak where you stand, or else I pull the cord."
   "Not unto thee, to Chiron there alone,
   Will we give answer,"—thus replied my lord:
   "Thy will to rashness ever more was prone."

Then, touching me, he said, " 'Tis Nessus,— look!
Who, for the beauteous Dejanira dying,
Himself full vengeance for his murder took.
Behold the middle one, his bosom eyeing, —
That is great Chiron, who Achilles bred;
And yon is Pholus, erst so full of ire.
By thousands thus about the streamlet's bed
They gallop, shooting each that riseth higher    72
Than his offence permits him to ascend."
As nearer to those agile beasts we drew,
Grim Chiron, with an arrow's feathered end,
Behind his jaws his long beard backward threw.
As thus his giant mouth the monster showed,
" Do ye perceive," he to his comrades said,
" The one behind, in walking shakes the road?
Not so are wont the footsteps of the dead."    80

Then my good Escort standing at his breast,
Where the two natures, fiend and beast, unite,
Replied: " I bring a solitary guest,
Alive, indeed, to show this vale of night.
Fated he comes; but not for pleasure's sake:
She from her heavenly hallelujahs came,
Who bade me this new duty undertake;
No robber he, nor I a soul of shame.    88

But by that virtue whence I venture thus
    Over a road so wild, so unexplored,
    One of thy band vouchsafe to go with us,
    And show us where the river we may ford;
And on his back this being let him take,
    Who is no spirit through the air to glide."
    Then towards his right breast Chiron turned and spake,
    Saying to Nessus, " Back! and be his guide.    96
Keep them aloof, if other troops you cross."
    So, onward with our trusty guard we went
    Along the brink of the red-seething fosse,
    Whence bitter shrieks the boiling wretches sent.

Up to their brows I saw them in the wave:
    " Tyrants those are," the mighty Centaur said,
    " Who their fell hearts to blood and plunder gave:
    Here, for their cruelties, vain tears they shed.    104
There's Alexander; Dionysius there,
    Long years of woe for Sicily who made;
    That forehead yonder, with the raven hair,
    Is Azzolino; that of lighter shade
Is Obyson of Este, whom 'tis true
    His step-son murdered in the world on high."
    I turned me to the bard, who said, " To you
    Be now the Centaur first — the second I."    112

## CANTO XII.

A little farther on, the Centaur stopped
   Over against a sunken people, shown
   To the throat only, which the stream o'ertopped:
   There one he pointed out, retired alone.
"He smote in God's own bosom," VIRGIL said,
   "The heart which men by Thamis yet revere."
   Then others I observed, who let the head
   And their whole chest above the tide appear.     120
Many I knew whom there I chanced to meet;
   And the ditch dwindled more and more away,
   Until it scarcely covered o'er the feet:
   Here o'er the bloody brook our passage lay.

"As on this side," the Centaur said, "thou see'st,
   More and more shallow still the streamlet grows,
   So upon this its depth is aye increased,
   Till back to where the tyrants groan it flows.     128
There divine Justice punishes the Kings
   Pyrrhus and Attila, earth's ancient scourge;
   And Sextus too; nay, tears eternal wrings, —
   By the sharp anguish of this boiling surge,
Eternal tears from Rinier Pazzo's eyes;
   And Rinier da Corneto, who of yore
   Filled all the highways with their butcheries."
Here he turned back, and crossed the ford once more.     136

## CANTO THE THIRTEENTH.

ERE Nessus had regained the other shore,
  We reached a desolate, untrodden wood:
  No verdant leaves, but inky black it bore;
  No smooth straight branches, but all gnarled and rude;
No fruit hung there, but only poisonous thorn.
  The savage beasts, that, in the wilderness
  Betwixt Corneto and the Cècina, scorn
  Farm-lands and fields, less rough a brake possess.    8
Amid the branches of this dismal grove,
  Their loathsome nests the brutal Harpies build,
  Who from the Strophades the Trojans drove
  With woful auguries ere long fulfilled.
Huge wings they have, men's faces, human throats,
  Feet armed with claws, vast bellies clothed with plumes:
  From those strange trees they pour their doleful notes.
  "Now, ere thou further penetrate these glooms,"    16

Said my good master, " thou shouldst understand
　Thou'rt in the second circlet, and shalt be,
　Until thou come upon the horrid sand.
　Give good heed then: more wonders thou shalt see,
Yea, to confirm all stories I have told."
　On every side I heard heart-rending cries,
　But not a person could I there behold;
　Wherefore I stopped, bewildered with surprise.　24
Methinks he thought I thought the voices came
　From some that, hiding, in the thicket lay:
　Because the Master said, " If thou but maim
　One of these plants, yea, pluck a branch away,
Then shall thy judgment be more just than now."
　Therefore my hand I slightly forward reached;
　And while I wrenched away a little bough
　From a huge bush, " Why mangle me ?" it screeched.　32
Then, as the dingy drops began to start,
　" Why dost thou tear me ?" shrieked the trunk again,
　" Hast thou no touch of pity in thy heart?
　We that now here are planted, once were men;
But, were we serpents' souls, thy hand might shame
　To have no more compassion on our woes:"
　Like a green log, that hisses in the flame,
　Groaning at one end, as the other glows, —　40
10

Even as the wind comes sputtering forth, I say,
  Thus oozed together from the splintered wood
  Both words and blood. I dropped the broken spray,
  And, like a coward, faint and trembling stood.
" O injured spirit!" thus replied my sage,
  " Could but this faithless mortal have believed
  What he hath read in my poetic page,
  He had not thus thy groaning fibres grieved.       48
I bade him, since thy fate belief transcends,
  Even though it pained myself, thy branches tear;
  That he on earth may make thee some amends.
Who wast thou? tell! — he will requite thee there:
Through him on high thy fame shall freshly shine."
  The trunk replied, " Thy pleasant words compel,
  As by a charm, my voice to answer thine.
  Oh, let me yield a little to the spell!       56

" Know I am he that once of Frederick's heart
  Held the two keys, and turned them as I chose,
  Opening and shutting it with such sweet art,
  He to none else his secrets would disclose.
In my high office with such zeal I burned,
  That my life's blood I made a sacrifice:
  But ah! the strumpet, — she who never turned
  From Cæsar's household her voluptuous eyes,       64

Envy, the common death and vice of courts,
　Kindled with hate of me the hearts of all,
　Who fired the Emperor so with false reports,
　That my glad honors turned to sorrow's gall.
Therefore my mind, resolving in disgust
　By death to 'scape disgrace and slander there,
　Made me, a just man, toward myself unjust;
　But, by this thorn-tree's new-grown roots, I swear        72
Never did I mine honored lord deceive:
　Should either of you from this world below
　Return to earth, let him my fame retrieve,
　Which mangled lies beneath fell Envy's blow."


The Poet waited for awhile, and then
　Said, " Lose no time, since he hath ended now:
　Wouldst thou hear further, question him again."
　" Rather," I answered him, " continue thou;—        80
Ask what thou think'st would satisfy me most;
　But I for very pity must forbear."
　Then VIRGIL thus: "O thou imprisoned ghost!
　So may this mortal freely grant thy prayer,
As thou to him shalt furthermore unfold
　How in these knots the tortured soul is bound;
　And if by any, from the cruel hold
　Of these gnarled limbs, escape is ever found."        88

Hereat the trunk heaved forth a heavy sigh,
    And soon these words articulate became:
    "To your inquiry take this brief reply:
When the mad soul tears off its bodily frame,
To the seventh gulf by Minos it is sped,
    And in this wood, where'er by fortune cast,
    Sprouts like a barley-corn, and rears its head,
    Grows to a sapling and wild plant at last.      96
The Harpies then, which on its foliage prey,
    Cause it to groan, and give its groans escape:
    We shall return, like others, for our clay;
    But none shall clothe him with his former shape.
Man ought to lose what he away hath flung:
    Hither our bodies we must drag to be
    Around this melancholy forest hung,
    Each on his guilty spirit's thorny tree."      104

We waited, thinking he had spoken more,
    When, as a hunter from his ambush sees
    The hunt rush headlong by, and frantic boar,
    And hears the noisy hounds and crashing trees,
Thus, at a sudden sound, we stood aghast;
    As, lo! two wretches from the left there drove,
    Shattering the impeding branches as they passed,
    Bleeding and scratched and naked through the grove.   112

" Death!"— cried the foremost, "to the rescue! fly!"
    The other, vexed that he less fleetly went,
    Cried, " Lano! not so nimbly didst thou ply
    Those legs of thine at Toppo's tournament."
Then, as if wanting wind, he stopped, and formed
    A single group there with a stunted plant;
    While close behind them all the forest swarmed
    With grim, black bitches, following fierce and gaunt.   120
Like greyhounds rushing from the leash, they darted,
    And, fastening on the wretch who lurking lay,
    Piecemeal his limbs with greedy fangs they parted,
    And bore the quivering fragments far away.

Then did mine Escort lead me toward the spot
    Where through its wounds the bramble vainly cried,
    " O Jacopo da Sant' Andrea! what
    Avails it thee behind my stem to hide?   128
Must I thy guilty life's just doom partake?"
    Hereat, my lord, pausing the trunk before,
    Said, " Who art thou, from whom at many a break
    Such bitter words come gushing with thy gore?"
He thus: " Ye spirits! who have come to see
    The shameful wreck which thus my leaves hath shred,
    Restore them to the foot of my sad tree.
    Know, in that city I was born and bred,   136

Which for the Baptist her first patron lost, —
    Mars; who for that shall work her every ill!
    And well for her, where Arno's wave is crossed,
    Some relic of him is remaining still,
Or else the citizens, who reared again
    The walls which Attila in ashes laid,
    Would have expended all their toil in vain.
    Of mine own roof-tree, I my gibbet made."

## CANTO THE FOURTEENTH.

My native land's dear memory had such force,
 That the strewn leaves I gathered from the ground,
 For him whom speaking now had rendered hoarse.
Then came we to the second circlet's bound,
 Where it is parted from the third; and here
 Justice a horrid vengeance hath contrived:
First then, to manifest these wonders clear,
 I say beside a sand-plain we arrived,
On whose waste bed no living stem there grows,
 Being encompassed by the woful wood,
 As round the wood the ditch of misery flows:
 Here, on its very verge, we pausing stood.
The soil was only one thick arid sand,
 Even like the shore by Cato's footsteps trod;
 Such was the semblance of this wretched land: —
 O thou dread vengeance of the Eternal God!

How shouldst thou thrill each mortal's heart with awe,
  Who reads what anguish there appalled mine eyes!
  Full many a herd of naked ghosts I saw,
  All howling hideously most piteous cries.
To these there seemed a various doom allotted;
  For some supine were stretched upon the ground,
  Others upon their haunches crouched and squatted,
  And some incessantly went round and round.
The latter formed more numerous a crowd
  Than those who down in agony had lain;
  But these were in their outcries far most loud.
  O'er all the sand slow fell a burning rain;
Wide-floating flakes of fire, resembling snow
  Among the Alps, when hushed is every flaw.
  As Alexander, where the sunbeams glow
  Hottest, in India, o'er his army saw
From heaven to earth the living cinders leap,
  And bade his soldiers trample on the ground,
  Lest, if allowed to gather in a heap,
  To quench them might more difficult be found;
So fell the eternal fire, which, as it lighted,
  To double their distress, inflamed the sands,
  Like tinder by the stricken steel ignited:
  Restless the motion was of wretched hands!

## CANTO XIV.

This way and that, as still they freshly fell,
  The scorching torments fast aside they brushed ;
  And I : " O Master ! thou, whose power could quell
All save the stubborn fiends who 'gainst us rushed, —
Those that opposed our entrance at the gate,
  Say, who is yonder prostrate giant, grim,
Writhing in scorn there of his fiery fate,
  As though this rain but served to harden him ? "   48


He then himself exclaimed, on hearing me
  Concerning him of my good guide inquire,
  " What once I was, continue I to be, —
In death as life. Though Jove his workman tire,
From whom he snatched the bitter bolt he threw
  At me, in rage, upon my day of doom ;
Though, one by one, he tire the others too,
  At the black furnace, down in Ætna's womb,   56
Crying, as erst he did at Phlegra's fight,
  ' Help me, good Vulcan ! help me, I entreat ! '
Yea, though he blast me with his fiercest might,
  Exult he may — but not in my defeat."
My leader hereupon more loudly spake
  Than ever I had heard his voice before :
" O Capaneus ! that pride of thine doth make, —
  That pride unquenchable, thy torment more.   64

No martyrdom save thine own fury, none,
  Could fitly match thy madness or thy crime."
  Then unto me more mildly: " That was one
  Of the seven kings at Thebes i'the olden time.
He had, and still he seemeth to retain,
  Small reverence for his God, even here in hell;
  But, as I said, that frenzy of disdain
  Torments him yet, his breast becoming well.        72

" But follow now behind me, — take good heed
  Lest in the burning sand thy feet thou set,
  And ever close beside the wood proceed."
So, silently we reached a streamlet's jet,
Down through the sand, forth from the forest rushing
  Whose crimson still I shudder to describe.
  Even like the brook from Bulicame gushing,
  Which the frail women share among their tribe;    80
So glided this: its pendent banks, its bed,
  And, on each hand, its margins, were of stone:
  So I perceived thereby our passage led.
" Of all the wonders I to thee have shown
Since first we passed the gate whose gloomy sill
  None is prohibited from entering o'er,
  Nought worthier notice than this present rill
  Has been presented to thine eyes before;          88

For over that the cinders all expire."
So spake my leader ; wherefore I besought,
That, having made me greedy with desire.
He might tell all I hungered to be taught.

" In the mid ocean spreads a dreary waste,"
He answered thus, — " a barren land, called Crete,
Under whose king the antique world lived chaste :
Therein Mount Ida lifts its lofty seat. 96
Once, in green gladness, full of springs, it rose ;
Now all deserted, as a thing outworn ;
This, for a faithful cradle, Rhea chose,
Where she might hide her little Jove, new-born.
So with wild shouts she drowned his infant cries :
Here hath a huge old form his mountain-home ;
His back towards Damiata turned ; his eyes,
As in a mirror, looking straight at Rome. 104
His head of fine gold is a shapen mass ;
Of purest silver are his arms and breast ;
Thence, to the middle, he is made of brass ;
Thence downward of choice iron all the rest, —
Save the right foot, which, rather than the left,
He stands erect on, — that is baked of clay ;
And every part, except the gold, is cleft
With a deep flaw, distilling tears for aye. 112

These gathering there, the stream a passage picks
  Through the dark grot, and down this valley leaps;
  Then forming first the Acheron and Styx
  And Phlegethon, through this close conduit creeps:
Thus ever sinking, till they can no more,
  The weary waters in Cocytus end;
  But of that famous fen I say no more,
  Thyself shalt witness it when we descend." 120

" If then," I answered, " as thy words assert,
  This rill a passage from our world hath found,
  Why first appears it on this sandy skirt?"
  " Thou know'st," he answered, " the abyss is round;
And though so far thou to the left hast strayed,
  Seeking the bottom of the infernal spheres,
  Not yet the circuit hast thou wholly made;
  So marvel not, if something new appears." 128
Then I: " O master! where is Lethe's tide?
  Where Phlegethon? — thou tellest nought of one,
  And say'st the other from that rain doth glide."
Said he, " Thy questions please me all, my son;
And yet the bubbling of that crimson wave
  Might have solved one: and Lethe thou shalt see
  Beyond this fosse, where spirits go to lave,
  When by repentance from their crimes set free. 136

But from the wood 'tis time we now retire:
Follow! and close behind my footsteps tread:
The banks afford a road secure from fire;
Over them too the vaporous flame is dead."

## CANTO THE FIFTEENTH.

ONE of that rivulet's hard, stony flanks
  Now forms our path: its gathering fumes o'ershade,
  And shield from fire, the water and its banks.
Such are the ramparts by the Flemings made
'Twixt Cadsand's isle and Bruges, lest the tide
  (Whose floods they fear) should their low country
    drown;
Or as the dikes that by the Brenta side
· The Paduans raise to fence each tower and town,
Ere Chiarentàna's top begins to warm,
  Such, though less large and lofty they appeared,
  Was of these solid banks the general form,
  Whatever master-hand the fabrics reared.

Already so far we had left the wood,
  That, had I turned about me, looking back,
  I could not have descried it whence I stood;
  When, lo! there met us, close beside our track,

A troop of spirits.  Each amid the band
   Eyed us, as men at eve a passer-by
   'Neath a new moon,— as closely us they scanned,
   As an old tailor doth his needle's eye.
One recognized me, of this tribe that gazed,
   And cried, the while he caught me by the gown,
   " What wonder's this ? "  So when his arm he raised,
   On his baked face I looked intently down.     24
Thus his burnt visage could not quite prevent
   His form from coming to my memory clear ;
   And, towards his features as my head I bent,
   I answered, " Ser Brunetto, are you here ? "

" O my dear son ! be not displeased," said he,
   " If old Brunetto from his train depart,
   And travel back a little way with thee."
   " That I entreat," said I, " with all my heart:    32
Nay, I'll sit with you, if he there advise
   With whom I go."— " Son, whoso of our band
   Stops but one instant, for a century lies
   Beat by this fire, unsheltered and unfanned.
Therefore move onward: to thy garment's hem
   I will but come,— then troop again with those,
   My sad companions, whom their crimes condemn
   To go bemoaning their eternal woes."     40

I, since I did not from our pathway dare
   Descend to him, inclined my drooping head,
   Like one that walks with reverential air.
Then he : " What destiny or chance hath led
Thee hither, ere thy final day, to rove ?
   And who is this that marshals thee the way ? "
   " In the serene existence there above,"
I answered, " in a vale, I went astray :
'Twas ere the fulness of mine age ; — I turned
   But yestermorn my back upon the glen ;
   Returning so, this being I discerned
Who by this road conducts me home again."

Then he : " If thou thy ruling star pursue,
   Thou shalt not fail a glorious port to win ;
   Else was my guess in life's fair scene untrue ;
   And, if my death had not so early been,
I, seeing thee so blest by heavenly grace,
   Thy lofty labor had myself befriended :
   But that ungrateful and malignant race
Who from Fiesole of yore descended,
   (Their flinty hearts retaining somewhat still
   Of that rough mount) thy virtue shall detest :
Good reason why — the dulcet fig but ill
   Can come to fruit by acrid sorbs oppressed.

CANTO XV. 89

Proud, envious people! greedy still of gain;
  Justly the old world's adage calls them blind:
  Of their vile customs wash thou off the stain;
  For thee great glory has thy Fate designed.
So shall each party hunger after thee;
  But far beyond the goat shall be the herb:
  On their own selves these beasts of Fesulæ
  May feed, but ne'er the nobler plant disturb,     72
If yet a single stem their dunghill bear,
  In whom the sacred seed appears anew
  Of those old Romans who yet lingered there,
  When of such wickedness the nest it grew."


" Might all my wish," I answered him, " be granted,
  Not yet hadst thou been banished humankind;
  Since the dear image in my heart implanted,
  Of thee, good father, still pervades my mind:     80
When in the world thou taught'st me, hour by hour,
  How man might make eternity his own;
  And evermore, while life permits the power,
  My gratitude shall in my song be shown.
Touching my fate, whatever you foretell
  I keep recorded, with another speech,
  For a blest maid, who will conceive and well
  Explain its meaning, if her side I reach.     88

12

Only to you be this resolve declared,
   So from my conscience be no blame incurred,
   Whatever Fortune wills, I stand prepared;
   Mine ears before have such forewarnings heard.
Whirl Fortune, then, her wheel as likes her best,
   And let the husbandman his mattock ply."
My Master, as my thought I thus expressed,
   Turned to his right, and fixed on me his eye:    96
" *He listeneth well who heedeth what he hears.*"
Thus VIRGIL: I, continuing to confer
With Ser Brunetto, asked, of his compeers
Who the most noted and important were.

" To know of some," he answered, " it is well;
   But silence best the others will beseem.
   Time were not long enough of each to tell;
   Yet know that all were clerks of great esteem;    104
Great scholars all, of whom Fame loudly talks;
   And all on earth one filthy sin defiled.
   There, with his hapless herd, lo! Priscian walks;
   Francesco too, is there, d'Accorso styled;
Yea, on a scab so loathsome wouldst thou look,
   Him thou mightst witness, whom, in sin grown rank,
   The Servants' Servant from the Arno took
   To hide away on Bacchiglione's bank :    112

There he was fain his ill-used nerves to leave.
   More I would speak of, but must needs refrain,
   Nor farther must I walk; for I perceive
   New smoke arising on the sandy plain.
Some other tribe this way their footsteps bend,
   From whose companionship I must forbear.
   To you, my son, my Treasure I commend,
   Wherein I yet survive — 'tis all my prayer." 120
Here, like a racer o'er Verona's plain
   For the green mantle, back again he ran;
   In speed resembling, as he flew amain,
   The winning, rather than the losing man.

## CANTO THE SIXTEENTH.

Now where I stood I heard the rumbling sound,
  Like swarms of bees that round their bee-hives hum,
  Of water falling to the other round:
  When towards us I beheld three spirits come.
Running, they sped together from a band
  Which passed beneath that martyrdom's rough showers,
  And each one shouted, " Ho, thou stranger, stand!
  Whose dress betrays that wicked land of ours."    8
Ah, me! upon their limbs what dreadful burns,
  What scars, both old and recent, shocked mine eye!
  Even yet my heart the mere remembrance yearns.
  And as my teacher listened to their cry,
" Wait," — whispered he, turning towards me his face,
  " One should use courtesy to such as they;
  But for the fearful nature of the place,
  Darting this fiery tempest, I might say    16

This eager haste less suited them than thee."
  Then, as we halted, they once more began
  Their ancient wail; and coming close, all three,
  With restless trot, round in a circuit ran.
As champions, oiled and naked for the fight,
  Are wont to watch their hold and vantage first,
  Ere in the deadly struggle they unite,
  Thus each at me his visage aimed reversed.   24
So foot and face went still in counterwise:


" And if," said one, " our aspect, parched and brown,
  And these tormenting sands, make thee despise
  Us and our prayers, yet reverence our renown;
And tell us, thou whose living feet are led
  Safely through Hell! who art thou? speak thy name.
  He, on whose footsteps thou perceiv'st I tread,
  Of nobler lineage than thou thinkest, came.   32
Yes: he so naked, even of skin bereaved,
  Was good Gualdrada's grandson, — even such;
  Great Guidoguerra, who in life achieved
  Much with his sword, and with his wisdom much.
And this, who next me walks the dreadful sand,
  Is one whose title in the upper air
  Should welcome be, — Tegghiaio Aldobrand!
  And I, their bitter agonies who share,   40

Was Rusticucci — chiefly let the blame
    Light on my savage wife for all my woe!"
    Hereat, had I been sheltered from the flame,
    Among them straight I would have leaped below.
My teacher, too, I think, had suffered this;
    But dread of scorching in that fiery place
    Conquered my wish, and forced me to dismiss
My greedy thirst to give them one embrace.

Then I began, " Soon as my Seignor, here,
    Uttered those words from which I rightly guessed
    That such a race as you were drawing near,
    Grief at your fate, not scorn, my soul possessed ;
And for long years that sorrow shall not perish.
    I am your countryman, and evermore
    Have loved your venerable names to cherish,
    And with affection conned your actions o'er.
Leaving the gall, I seek the pleasant fruit
    Promised to me by this my truthful guide ;
    But to the centre first must sink my foot."
" So may thy spirit lead thy limbs!" he cried :
" So shine thy fame, too, after thee! as thou
    Shalt answer this: within our city's wall
    Dwells Courtesy as once, and Valor now?
    Or are those virtues cast aside by all?

For William Borsière, he who herds,
   A recent comer here, — in yonder crowd,
   Torments us greatly with his bitter words."
Hereat I raised my face, and cried aloud,
" O upstart race! — the sudden growth of gain
   Hath bred such inequality in thee,
   Such pride, O Florence! well mayst thou complain."
Receiving which for answer, all the three      72
Looked at each other with such conscious eyes
   As men who hear truth told, — then answered thus:
   " Oh, happy thou! might always thy replies
Cost thee no more than this free speech to us!
And shouldst thou ever from this dismal air
   Return to view the lovely stars again,
   When thou shalt say with pleasure, 'I was there;'
Recall our names, and speak of us to men."      80
The circle then immediately was broken;
   Their nimble legs seemed wings, so swift they darted:
   The word "Amen" could scarcely have been spoken
So quick as from my vision they departed.

My master now thought best to journey on:
   I followed; and the murmur grew so near
   Of the cascade, that, ere we far had gone,
Even our own voices we could hardly hear.      88

Like to that rill, in channel of its own,
   The first from Monte Veso, flowing east,
   Down the left coast of Apennine, and known
   Above as Acquacheta, till increased,
The waters bed themselves in level shores,
   And by Forli that name no longer keep;
   As there above Saint Benedict it roars,
Bounding, at one fall, down an Alpine steep,
Where for a thousand might have been supply;
   Thus down a rugged precipice we found
   That dingy torrent rushing from on high,
   Palsying our ears with its perpetual sound.

I had a cord about my body tied,
   Wherewith I formerly had thought to noose
   The leopard, shining in the dappled hide;
   Which thus my guide commanded me to use:
First having freed me from this girdle quite,
   I reached it, gathered in a coil, to him;
   Then he, a little veering towards the right,
   Cast it a certain distance from the brim
Of the rough rock, adown the steep abyss.
   Some wonder now methought will soon reply
   Unto a signal new and strange as this,
   Which thus my master seconds with his eye.

Ah, with what caution men should aye proceed
  With those who look not merely at men's works,
  But, with their intellectual vision, read
  Each hidden thought which in the bosom lurks!
Here VIRGIL spake, " Full quickly from below
  That which I watch for and thy fancy dreams
  Will to thy wondering sight its figure show."
From uttering truth which like a falsehood seems,     120
The lip of man should evermore forbear,
  Lest he be shamed, though innocent of wrong :
  But here I must speak boldly; and I swear
  To thee, O reader, by this sacred song!
So may the fame thereof for aye endure, —
  That a strange figure swimming met my gaze,
  Up through that thickest atmosphere obscure,
  To smite the steadiest bosom with amaze :     128
As one who dives to set an anchor free,
  Grappling with some huge rock in ocean's bed,
  Or other clog that lurks beneath the sea,
  Returns with feet drawn in and arms outspread.

## CANTO THE SEVENTEENTH.

"BEHOLD the beast of the sharp tail, who breaks
  Through arms and walls! who passeth mountains, — yea,
  Foul with his stench the whole creation makes!"
Thus unto me began my guide to say,
And beckoning up the monster to the brim,
  Nigh to the marble causeway's craggy close,
  Straight at the sign, Fraud's image, foul and grim,
  Both head and bosom, from the gulf arose;      8
All save his end, — he drew not that ashore:
  Fair as an honest man's appeared his face,
  So smooth and gracious an outside he wore;
  But all the rest was of the serpent race.
Two branching limbs he had, with shaggy hair
  From the paws even to the armpits decked:
  His breast, his back, and both flanks everywhere
  With painted knots and little rings were specked.    16

Never with more variety of shade,
  By any Tartar artisans or Turks,
  Was web of cloth inwoven or o'erlaid,
  Nor with more hues Arachne wove her works.
As barges oft lie drawn upon the strand,
  Partly ashore and partly in the tide;
  And even as, in the greedy German's land,
  The beaver, ambushing for prey doth hide, —            24
Such was that vilest brute's insidious mode:
  While on the sand-waste's rocky rim he clung;
  In the void chasm his wriggling tail he showed,
  As up the envenomed, forked point he swung,
Which, as in scorpions, armed its tapering end.
  And thus my guide: " Towards yon perfidious beast,
  Our pathway now must for a little bend,
  Where on the brink he crouches, as thou seest."       32

So to the right, descending from the ledge
  More fairly to avoid the sand and flame,
  We took ten paces on the abyss's edge,
  And closer still to that dread creature came.
Now, farther on that desert, I discern,
  Nigh to the void, some seated on the ground;
  And here my lord: " That thou mayst fully learn
  The nature and condition of this round,                40

Go forward there, and witness their distress;
　But let thy parley with them be but short:
　Till thy return, this beast I will address,
　And ask for us his shoulder's strong support."
So farther still, upon the utmost bourne
　Of that Seventh Circle, all alone I strayed,
　Where sat the wretches doomed for aye to mourn:
　O, how their eyes their agonies betrayed! 48
Ever by turns against the fiery sleet
　And the hot sand, their swift hands they employed;
　As dogs in summer ply both jaws and feet,
　By the fell brize or flies or fleas annoyed.

Then, as on certain forms I fixed mine eyes,
　On whom the torment of that fire was flung,
　I marked, although I none could recognize,
　From each one's neck a money-bag was hung, 56
Each purse a blazon bore and special hue
　Which seemed, as 'twere, their gloating gaze to nurse;
　And, as I came among them, met my view
　An azure emblem on a yellow purse:
A lion's face and bearing it displayed;
　And onward still as rolled mine orb of sight,
　Redder than blood another I surveyed,
　Which bore a goose, like whitest butter white. 64

And one, whose emblem was a teeming sow
  Emblazoned azure on an argent pouch,
  Cried, "In this devil's ditch, what seekest thou?
  Begone! yet first attend what I avouch:
Know thou, since life remaineth still to thee,
  Vitaliano, once my neighbor nigh,
  Shall sit here shortly on the left of me —
  Amongst these Florentines, a Paduan I:  72
And oftentimes they thunder in mine ear,
  'Soon with his wallet and three goats displayed
  O, come along our sovran cavalier!'"
Grimaces then with mouth and tongue he made,
Licking his nostril, as an ox is wont;
  And I departed from the weary throng,
  Fearful by more delaying to affront
  Him who had warned me not to linger long.  80

I found my leader there already planted
  Fast on the flank of that detested brute;
  And thus he said: "Be strong now, and undaunted!
  Such are the stairs that our descent must suit.
Mount thou in front, — myself will midway sit,
  Lest the tail harm thee." As a mortal, shook
  By the near visit of an ague's fit,
  Who shudders even on the shade to look,  88

His nails already corpse-like with the cold,—
Such I became, his dreadful words to hear;
Till shame, which makes a timid servant bold
Before his good lord's frown, rebuked my fear.

So, as he counselled me, I took my place
   On those huge shoulders, and I strove to say,
   Do thou but steady me with thy embrace;
But terror took all power of speech away.
He then, who many a time and oft before,
   On great occasion, helped me at my need,
   With his arm girdling me, my weight upbore,
   And cried aloud, "Now, Geryon, proceed!
Take ample sweep — be gradual thy descent:
A novel fraught thou bearest — gently sink!"
Like a small vessel from its moorage went
That monster, backing, backing from the brink.
And when he found that he could freely wheel,
   He turned about his outstretched tail to where
His breast had been, moving it like an eel,
   And with his great paws gathered in the air.

I doubt if Phaeton more wild became
   With terror, when he let the bridle go,
   And Heaven's vault kindling, caught the sudden flame
Whereof the skies even yet some token show;

Or hapless Icarus, when first he felt
  (The whilst his father cried, "Thou steer'st amiss!")
  The wax beginning from his wings to melt,
  Than I, thus launched upon the void abyss.
Nought but the beast was possible to view:
  He slowly, slowly wound in many a curve;
  Though only from a wind, which upward blew
  Against my face, his course I could observe. 120
Down on the right, I heard the whirlpool seethe,
  Where splashing fell the horrible cascade;
  And, straining forth my neck to gaze beneath,
  At the dread plunge I grew still more afraid.
Such groans I heard, and saw such glare of fires,
  Whereat I shrunk, all quivering with affright;
  And marked his manner of descent, in spires,
  Which until now the darkness kept from sight. 128

Now, on each side, new horrors I survey;
  And like a hawk, that scouring long the skies,
  Without discovering either lure or prey,
  Till, "Ha, thou'rt faltering!" the vexed falc'ner cries, —
As tired he sinks to where he started, light,
  And, in a hundred whirls careering round,
  Perches disdainfully, and full of spite,
  Far from his lord, at last upon the ground, 136

So Geryon, stooping, set us on our feet
　　Down at the base of that rude cliff abhorred;
　　And straight, disburthened, bounded off as fleet
As ever sped an arrow from a cord.

## CANTO THE EIGHTEENTH.

HELL hath a region Malebolge called,
   All rock and iron-coloured, like the steep
   Wherewith around the wicked fold is walled:
   A well yawns through its centre wide and deep.
In its due order I shall speak of this;
   But for that girdle which remains between
   The precipice's foot and the abyss,
   To part the space ten trenches intervene.     8
As where some castle to defend from storm
   Moats after moats beyond the walls appear,
   Giving the land there its peculiar form,
   Such was the fashion of these hell-pits here.
And in such fortresses as bridges cross
   From the tower's threshold to the farther bank,
   So from the cliff's base rocks arched every fosse,
   From brink to brink, till in the well they sank:     16

The great chasm cuts and gathers all at last;
  And in this realm, when Geryon from his back
  Had shaken us, the Poet straightway passed
  To the left hand, I following still his track.

Now on my right new miseries pained my view,
  Another kind of scourgers was employed,
  And the first trench was filled with torments new;
  Two ranks of naked sinners paced the void:
Tow'rds us advancing came the nearer band;
  The farther strode more rapidly along,
  The way we went: the Romans thus have planned
  To regulate the passage of the throng
When, on the Year of Jubilee, each train,
  By reason of such numbers, keeps one side;
  One towards the castle and Saint Peter's fane
  Pouring, the other towards the mount doth glide.
All o'er the dun rock scattered I could see
  Demons with horns; each plied a mighty whip,
  Lashing them sorely on their backs — ah me,
  How the first sting made those poor sinners skip!
None stayed a second nor a third, but fled;
  And still proceeding, lo! amid the swarm
  One I observed of whom I quickly said
  " Mine eyes ere now have feasted on that form!"

And fixed my gaze his features to retrace,
  While my dear leader lingered at my side,
  Nay, suffered me to wander back a pace
  Towards the flayed wretch that vainly sought to hide.
Vainly he hung his head for I exclaimed,
  " Thou art Venètico — although thine eyes
  Avoid my look — Caccianimico named!
  Unless that face thy actual self belies.        48
But what has brought thee to this bitter cup?"
  " To tell," he answered, " I am ill inclined,
  But must, for thy clear accent conjures up
  The dear old world's remembrance to my mind.
'Twas I the beauteous Isola betrayed
  To the vile Marquis, his desire to please,
  However else that shameful tale be said:
  Nor weep I here the only Bolognese;        56
So swarms this crowded region with our ranks,
  That fewer living tongues say 'sipa' now
  Betwixt Savena's and the Reno's banks:
  Wouldst be assured thereof, remember thou
How deeply avarice in our nature grows."
  While thus he spake a demon drove him on
  With his fell whip, crying, betwixt the blows,
  " Pandar! — no women to let here — begone!"        64

I left the wretch and now rejoined my guide:
  Only a few steps brought us where extended
  One of those rocks that jut from the bank side
  Which we full nimbly to the right ascended.
Up o'er the crag continuing thus our march,
  We left those everlasting rounds of woe
  And reached the summit where it forms an arch
  For the scourged multitude to pass below.  72
" Stop," said my leader; " let this other crew
  Of ill-starred miscreants thy full vision strike,
  Whose faces have not fairly met thy view,
  Seeing our course and theirs were both alike."

From the old bridge the sinners we beheld
  Toward us advancing now, that adverse band,
  In the same manner by the lash compelled;
  And thus my lord, ere I could make demand,  80
" Observe yon mighty one that, 'mid the train,
  For all his misery seems no tear to shed:
  How much his features yet the king retain!
  'Tis Jason, basely both with heart and head
Who robbed the Colchians of their fleece of gold:
  Fast by the Lemnian isle he set his sails,
  When the fierce women, pitiless and bold,
  Had slain by savage compact all their males.  88

There with love-gifts and passion well profest
  Hypsipyle, young virgin, he beguiled,
  Who had herself deluded all the rest;
  Then full of grief he left her, and with child.
Such condemnation for such crime is meet;
  Here too Medea's wrong he must atone:
  With him go all who practise like deceit.
  Enough of this first valley now is known;              96
Enough of those whom that fierce torment rends."
  Now came we where our pathway's narrow ridge
  Across the second boundary's rim extends
  Which serves as buttress to another bridge.

Thence heard we people in the trench beneath
  Who sadly moaning, slap themselves full sore,
  And through their mouths and nostrils chokedly breathe.
  With a foul mould the sides were crusted o'er;        104
Exhaling from below, it clung thereto
  Offering annoyance both to smell and sight:
  So deep the den its bottom none might view,
  Save from the rocky bridge's topmost height.
Hither we came, and in the pit below
  I saw a multitude in ordure drowned
  Which seemed from human reservoirs to flow;
  And, as with searching eye I peered around,           112

One with a head so loaded I descried
  'Twere hard to say if priest or layman he;
  " Wherefore so much more greedily," he cried,
  " Than these my brother brutes regard'st thou me?"
" Because," I said, " unless my memory stray,
  I've seen thee with dry locks more neatly drest:
  Thou'rt a Lucchese — Alessio Interminei!
  Therefore I mark thee more than all the rest."    120

He mumbled, thumping on his pumpkin pate,
  " Flattery, whereof my tongue had ne'er its fill,
  Thus low hath sunk me to this loathsome fate."
  Hereat my guide — " Gaze farther onward still;
A little farther, till thy vision meet
  Yonder loose harlot, squalid and obscene,
  Who croucheth now, now riseth on her feet,
  And often tears herself with nails unclean.    128
Tis the lewd Thäis who made answer thus,
  When her swain asked her if her thanks were great:
  ' O yes! — my gratitude is marvellous!'
  And here be this enough our gaze to sate."

## CANTO THE NINETEENTH.

O Simon Magus!—O ye wretches led
 By him! who still the gifts of Heaven's great Sire,
 Which should alone with holiness be wed,
 Make prostitute for gold and silver hire.
Now must the trumpet sound for you! whose doom
 Is this third pit—Ascending now again
 We came above the next succeeding tomb
 Where the crag spans the middle of the den.    ⁸
Wisdom supreme! what wondrous art in Heaven,
 On earth, and in the wicked world is shown—
 What just allotment has thy goodness given!
 I saw the surface of the livid stone
O'er side and bottom pierced with many a hole
 Of equal size, and every hole was round;
 Such as about the great baptismal bowl
 Are in my beautiful Saint John's Church found;   ¹⁶

(No less nor larger they appeared to me)
    One of which holes, not many years ago,
    I brake to set a stifled creature free;
    Let all the truth by this avowal know.

Forth from each mouth a sinner's quivering feet
    And legs protruded, far as to the calf —
    Both soles afire! burning with fiercest heat —
    Buried within remained the other half. 24
Such fearful spasms the ancle-joints o'ercame,
    The force had sundered withes and ropes to shreds:
    As when Anointed things are burnt, the flame
    Swims o'er the surface first and flickering spreads,
Even such this blaze appeared, from toe to heel.
    "Master," I asked, "what wretch is writhing there,
    With greater anguish than his comrades feel,
    Sucked by that flame of a more sanguine glare?" 32
He answered; "I will bear thee, if thou wilt,
    Down there, by yon more gradual decline,
    So shalt thou learn from him his name and guilt."
    And I to him, "Thy pleasure still is mine;
Thou art my lord, thou know'st my silent thought,
    And knowest from thy will I never stray."
    Me then he straight on that fourth causeway brought,
    And leftward turning, we pursued our way 40

Down to the pent and perforated space ;
  Nor did he from his hip set down my load
  Till he had borne me to the open place
  Through which that sinner's limbs his anguish shewed.

" Whoe'er thou art, O spirit full of woe !
  That in this rock, thus planted like a stake,
  Art doomed to hold thine upper part below,
  If thou canst utter aught, some answer make."
I stood confessor-like (in act to shrive
  Some vile assassin who, his feet in air,
  Calls back the friar, to linger still alive)
And he cried out — " Ha, Boniface ! art there ?
Thou, standing there ! already come to fate ?
  The writing then by several years hath lied :
  So soon thy soul could that possession sate
  For which thou did'st beguile the beauteous bride
Thenceforth by thee so cruelly abused ? "
  Here I became like those who vainly seek
  To comprehend some answer, all confused
  As if bemocked, unknowing what to speak.

Then Virgil thus ; " Reply without delay
  I am not he, not he thou hast believed."
  Therefore I answered as he bade me say,
  The spirit writhing both his feet as grieved.

Sighing he asked, in accents moaning low,
  " Desir'st thou aught of me ? — what wouldst thou then ?
  Know, if it so concern thy soul to know
That thou hast ventured to explore this den,
  I the great mantle wore and was indeed
  A true Orsini, whelp of that She-bear
Whose cubs I strove to advance, with such good speed
  That I'm bagged here as I bagged money there. 72
Headlong beneath my head are buried more,
  Crammed in this rock's inexorable chink,
  Who practised simony like me before :
So I, in my turn, farther down shall sink ;
Ay, soon as he approacheth whom my tongue
  Hastily greeted, as I thought, in thee ;
  But I reversed, with burning soles, have hung
Longer than he, with his, shall planted be. 80
For after him shall follow, from the West,
  A lawless pastor, uglier far of deed,
  By whom we both shall farther down be prest ;
One of whose like in Maccabees we read ;
Another Jason, whom his king of old
  Favored as this one He whom France obeys."
I know not here but I was over-bold
  That thus I ventured my reply to phrase ; 88

"What sum now, tell me, did our Lord demand,
  In the first instance, and how large a fee,
  IIis keys consigning to Saint Peter's hand?
  Surely he asked no more but — 'Follow me!'
Nor gold nor silver Peter and the rest
  Asked of Matthias, when the lot he drew
  For that high place which Judas had possest;
  Therefore remain! thy doom is justly due:
Take thou good care of that ill-gotten gain
  Which boldened thee to join 'gainst Charles in strife,
  And did not reverence my tongue restrain
  For the high charge thou held'st in joyous life —
Those mighty keys which were of yore thine own —
  I could have spoke in terms more bitter still:
  Your avarice makes the universe to groan,
  Trampling down good men and exalting ill;
The Evangelist, ye priests! had sight of you,
  When she that, born with seven heads, commits
  Whoredom with kings was present to his view —
  The one that over many waters sits —
She that in sign of power ten horns displayed,
  While yet her spouse the ways of virtue sought:
  Your God of gold and silver ye have made!
  Differs the idolater from you in aught

Save that he worships one and hundreds ye?
  Ah, Constantine! to how much ill gave birth
  Not thy conversion, but that dower by thee
  Given the first Pope whose treasure was of earth!

And while I sang to him in such a strain,
  Whether it were by conscience stung or rage,
  Both of his blazing soles he writhed amain;
  Which I believe well pleased my guiding sage,     120
Since ever with so satisfied a look
  He listened to the truths my words expressed.
  My body then with both his arms he took
  And when he had me wholly on his breast,
Remounted by the way he held before,
  Nor slacked his grasp, as wearied with his charge,
  But to the archway's top my burden bore
  Which joins the fourth to the succeeding marge.     128
Here gently down my master set his load,
  Gently, for steep and rugged was the height,
  Which very goats had found no easy road:
  Thence a new trench lay open to my sight.

## CANTO THE TWENTIETH.

Now of new punishment I have to sing,
  And more material for the twentieth strain
  Of this first portion of my poem bring,
  The part which treats of people sunk in pain.
I stood already gazing, eager-eyed,
  Down the disclosed abyss, which overflowed
  With woful tears, and there a race descried
  Who towards us through the trenched circuit strode.     8
Silent and weeping, with the solemn gait
  Of men who chant the litanies they came;
  And, as mine eye more closely scanned their state,
  Strangely reversed appeared each sinner's frame.
Twisted where neck doth chin and chest unite,
  High o'er their loins their visages they held;
  Having before them thus no power of sight,
  To walk with backward step they were compelled.     13

Perhaps, ere now, by palsy's powerful touch,
　Some wretch there may have been so wrenched about
　But, for myself, I never witnessed such,
　And if one ever were, I greatly doubt.
Think reader now, — God only grant thou reap
　Good from thy reading! — how could I so near
　Behold our form distorted thus and keep
　These cheeks of mine unmoistened with a tear?　　　21
For, down the channel of their backs there crept
　Rivers of tears; so that I leaned beside
　One of the splinters of the rock, and wept;
　For which reproved me thus my kindly guide:

"Art thou, too, like the rest, bereft of sense?
　Here piety most lives when pity dies.
　What guilt can greater be than his offence
　Who views God's justice with compassion's eyes?　　　32
Lift, lift thine head! at him look yonder now
　For whom earth opened in the Thebans' sight
　While all exclaimed, — 'Ha! whither rushest thou,
　Amphiaràus? — why forsake the fight? —'
Meanwhile he fell, in hopeless ruin, far
　As Minos, monarch of the all-seizing clutch:
　See how his bosom now his shoulders are!
　Once he would fain have forward seen too much:　　　40

Therefore he backward walks, with eyes behind.
   Behold Tiresias next, the Seer who took
   A female shape, yea, wholly changed his kind,
   Wearing a woman's limbs, a woman's look,
And his male plumage ere he could restore
   Needs must he use again his magic rod
   And strike therewith those coupling snakes once more:
   Aruns comes after, doomed like him to plod.    48

'Mid the white marbles, up in Luni's hills,
   Whose sides the peasant, nestling at their base,
   Down in the village of Carrara, tills,
   He had a cavern for his dwelling place:
Thence he could gaze, with nought his eye to check
   From gazing on the stars and on the sea.
   But look at her whose dangling tresses deck
   Her breast that is not visible to thee:    56
Behold how all her hair before her grows!
   Manto she was, who searched through many a clime
   Till in my birth-place she obtained repose;
   Wherefore I pray thee listen for a time.
After the maiden's royal Father died,
   When Bacchus' town a tyrant's thrall became,
   Long through the world she wandered far and wide.
   Up in fair Italy a lake, by name    64

Benacus, lies, beneath those Alps which, o'er
    The Tyrol soaring, Germany impale :
    A thousand fountains, I believe, and more,
    Bathe Appenine 'twixt Garda and the vale
Camonica, then slumber in that lake :
    Hard by, Trent's bishop and Verona's might,
    With Brescia's too, if they that way should take,
    Their benediction give with equal right.    72
Where wider space the sloping shore permits,
    The Bergamese and Brescians to confront,
    A strong and sightly hold, Peschiera sits :
Here swoln Benacus to o'erflow is wont,
And forms a stream whereby the meads are crossed ;
    But when the waves a headlong river grow
    Their name Benacus is in Mincius lost,
    Far as Governo, where it falls in Po.    80
Soon in its course the current finds a bed
    Spreading o'er which, it settles to a marsh
    Whence oft in summer pestilence is bred :
Hither she came, this virgin sad and harsh ;
And finding in the middle of the fen
    A vacant waste, all desolate and bare,
    Yearning to shun all intercourse with men,
    She stopped and fixed her habitation there.    88

Here with her slaves she plied her wicked arts,
  But left her body tenantless at length:
  Then people, scattered round the neighboring parts,
  Gathered thereto as to a place of strength,
(Being on all sides by the marsh protected)
  And over her dead bones a city walled;
  The which, from her who first the spot selected,
  Without more augury, they Mantua called.    96
Ere Casalodi's foolishness had been
  By Pinamonte's artifice deceived,
  Its walls a greater multitude shut in:
  I charge thee be this true account believed,
Whatever false narration thou mayst hear,
  Of my land's origin," — I thus replied;
  " Master my faith in thee is so sincere
  In thy relation I must needs confide;    104
All other tales dead embers are to me:
  But tell me now, of those that onward go,
  Any of notice worthy dost thou see?
  For that alone my mind is bent to know."

" He," Virgil answered, " from whose cheek there trails
  A beard o'er shoulders of a dusky hue,
  Was once, when Greece was so bereft of males
  That even the cradles hardly held a few,    112

The soothsayer Eurypylus, the same,
  In Aulis, who with Calchas gave the sign
  For the first cable to be cut; his fame
  Lives in that lofty tragic verse of mine:
Thou well know'st where who knowest all my strain.
  That other yonder, round the loins so small,
  Was Michael Scott, who truly could explain
  The magic art with its impostures all.     120
See Guy Bonatti! on Asdente look!
  Repenting now sincerely, but too late,
  That e'er his thread and leather he forsook
  To meddle with the mysteries of fate.
Behold those wretched women that resigned
  Spindle and shuttle for more dangerous arms;
  Who threw aside their needles and divined,
  With herbs and images contriving charms.     128

But come: already close to the confines
  Of either hemisphere the wanderer, Cain
  Comes with his thorn-bush, and his orb declines
  Low under Seville, dipping in the main.
The moon thou know'st was rounded yesternight:
  Thou shouldst remember well how oft she shone,
  Through the deep wood, to aid thee with her light."
Thus he to me: meanwhile we travelled on.     136

## CANTO THE TWENTY-FIRST.

With other talk pursuing thus our march,
 But what, my comedy cares not to say,
 We reached the top of the succeeding arch,
 And paused, another fissure to survey.
More vain laments here Malebolge breathes;
 And dark it looked — yea, wondrously obscure.
 Like sticky pitch, that during winter seethes,
 In the Venetians' arsenal, to cure
Their wounded ships — for, since the time prevents
 Their navigation, in that leisure one
 Rebuilds his bark, another calks the rents
 In some old hull that many a course hath run;
O'er bow, o'er stern, the busy hammerers bend,
 Some fashion oars, and some huge cables twine,
 And some the mizzen, some the mainsail mend —
So, not by force of fire, but art divine,

Down underneath, a thick tar boiled and swelled,
  Wherewith on either side the bank was smeared.
  I saw the liquid, but therein beheld
  Nought but the bubbles which the boiling reared:
I saw it heave and then, comprest, subside:
  And while I gazed intently as I could
  Down in the den — " Beware!" my leader cried,
  And drew me toward himself from where I stood.   24

I turned — like one who lingers to behold
  Something that seen might well persuade his flight,
  Yet, as his blood with sudden fear grows cold,
  Checks not his speed to satisfy his sight, —
And saw a fiend, not far behind our back,
  Rushing up towards us o'er the rocky road;
  How fell his aspect was! how fierce and black!
  And oh, what cruelty his gesture shewed!   32
Swiftly, with outspread wings, he skimmed his way;
  Across his high and peaked shoulder cast,
  A sinner's carcase on both haunches lay,
  The fiend the ancle-sinew griping fast.
" Ye of our bridge," he cried, " curst-claws! I bear
  One of Saint Zita's elders in my clutch:
  Plunge him down deep, and back I will repair
  To fetch you more — his land breeds plenty such.   40

There, save Bonturo, every man's a cheat;
  There yes of no for money they can make" —
  Hurling him down, back o'er the hard rock, fleet
He sped like a mastiff set some thief to take.
The sinner plunged, then doubled up arose,
  While underneath the bridge more demons cried,
  " No Sacred Visage Malebolge knows —
  Far different swimming this from Serchio's tide!  48
Unless by our fell forks thou wouldst be maimed,
  Look lest thou get above the pitch by chance."
  More than a hundred prongs at him they aimed,
  Crying; " Here under cover thou must dance!
So, if thou'rt able, do thy filching hid;"
  And struck him down as cunningly as cooks,
  Lest the meat rise above the cauldron, bid
Their scullions keep it under with their hooks.  56

Then my good master, " Lest it should be seen
  That thou art here, conceal thee and crouch down
  Behind this rock, and let it be thy screen.
  Whate'er they threat me, fear thou not their frown:
Well I foreknow their conduct and th' event,
  Having before endured as fierce a brunt."
  Then down the bridge to the sixth bank he went
Where needed he to wear a fearless front.  64

With equal fury and such storm of wrath
  As when dogs fly some loiterer to attack,
  Who stops and cries for alms upon his path,
Rushed from beneath the bridge the spiteful pack,
And against him their weapons pointed all;
  But Virgil cried: "Let none his rage display.
  Ere on my form you let your flesh-hooks fall,
  Come forward one and hear what I would say;    72
Let him consider then of striking me."
  The fiends all shouted: "Malacoda, go!"
  Whereat one moved: the rest remaining, he
Came growling on: "What brings thee here below?"

"Believ'st thou Malacoda, thou hadst here,"
  My master said, "seen me, despite your hate,
  Walk from all harm secure and void of fear,
  Without the will divine and favouring fate?    80
Through this wild way this mortal's feet to guide
  Heav'n grants me power—dare not my course to stop!"
  Straight at these words so fell the demon's pride
Down at his feet he let his hell-fork drop,
"We must not strike him;" saying to the rest.
  My leader then — "O thou, who cowerest there
  Amid the splinters of the bridge comprest,
  Hither to me securely now repair."    88

So scrambling forth, I sped me to his side
   Yet, as the devils their advance renewed,
   Shuddered lest by their truce they might not bide:
   So shook the infantry that once I viewed,
When they by compact from Caprona came,
   To see themselves hemmed round so by their foes;
   And clinging to my guide with all my frame,
   I gazed and could not move my gaze from those. 96
No trait of goodness tempered their bad looks:
   " Wouldst thou"—growled one, " I hit him on the hip ?"
   The others answered, aiming down their hooks,
   " Ay, fork him, fellow ! let him feel it nip."
But he, the fiend that with my leader spake,
   Cried, turning quick: "Stay, Scarmiglione, stay!"
   Then unto us: " No farther can you take
   In this direction o'er these crags your way: 104
All ruined lies the sixth arch to the base ;
   If 'tis your object onward to proceed
   Along this margent ye must keep your pace ;
   Hard by another rock will serve your need.
For know, that yesterday, five hours more late
   Than this self hour, twelve hundred rolling years
   Threescore and six fulfilled the course of fate,
   Since here the way was shattered as appears. 112

Thither I send this brigad of my crew
  To mark if any peer above the scum:
  Go with them — harmless they shall be to you:"
  Then he began: " Come, Alichino, come !
Come Calcabrina — and Cagnazzo thou !
  And Barbariccia ! thou the ten shalt lead:
  Now Libicocco — Draghinazzo now !
  Fanged Ciriatto — Graffiacane speed !
Mad Rubicante — Farfarello — march !
  And round about the boiling pitch explore:
  These give safe conduct far as that next arch,
  Which all entire the caverns crosseth o'er."


" O master mine ! " said I, " what is't I see ?
  Alone let us, without an escort go:
  I ask none, if the way be known to thee:
  Look at yon grinning fiends ! what tusks they show !
Markest thou not, if prudence rule thee still,
  With what a menace those fell brows are bent ? "
  " Fear not," he answered, " let them snarl at will;
  'Tis for their seething victims only meant."
By the left bank the fiendish cohort veered;
  But each his tongue first pressed his teeth between,
  And with this signal at their leader leered;
  Who blew a bugle-note of sound obscene.

## CANTO THE TWENTY-SECOND

I HAVE, ere now, seen cavalry shift camp,
  Begin the assault, and muster in array;
  And sometimes in retreat with rapid tramp:
Light horsemen o'er your fields have I seen play,
Ye Aretines! and squadrons as they passed,
  The clash of tournaments and tilting knights,
  Sometimes with drums and oft with trumpet blast,
  And bells and signals given from castle heights,     8
With foreign instruments and with our own;
  But horse or foot I never saw before
  Moving to music of so strange a tone,
  Nor ship by any sign of star or shore.

With those ten fiends we went. Ah troop of sin!
  Fearful companionship! but ever so —
  With saints at church, with gourmands at an inn:
Yet I gazed only at the pitch below;     16

Bent all the contents of that den to view,
And who those might be scalding there inside :
And like as dolphins warn a watchful crew
Means for their vessel's safety to provide,
By their arched backs, that coming storms forebode,
So, to relieve the torture's keen extreme,
At times his back a quivering sinner showed,
Then vanished quicker than the lightning's gleam.
And just as frogs that stand, with noses out
On a pool's margin, but beneath it hide
Their feet and all their bodies but the snout,
So stood the sinners there on every side.
But soon as Barbariccia drew more near,
Under the bubbles ducked they down full swift :
I witnessed then what thrills me yet with fear,
One lingering longer, with his head uplift —
As one frog stays, while darts the next away —
And Graffiacane, being nearest, hooked
Forth by the tarry locks his writhing prey :
Like a speared otter to my sight he looked.

I knew each demon's appellation now,
For when selected, I had marked them well,
And when one hailed his mate, I noticed how :
Then thus I heard them all together yell.

"O Rubicante! fix those claws of thine
  So in his back that thou his carcase flay!"
Then I: "If thou art able, master mine,
  Inform thyself concerning him I pray:
Who is the luckless wretch that thus hath chanced
  The clutch of such keen enemies to bide?"
Close to his side my leader then advanced,
  Saying: "Whence camest thou?" And he replied:  48

"Navarre's proud kingdom was my native place:
  My mother put me in a lord's employ,
For she had borne me to a spendthrift base,
  Bent both himself and substance to destroy.
The good king Tybalt next I served, and here
  To peculation all my thoughts I turned,
For which I render an account so dear,
  In this hot punishment where I am burned."  56
Then Ciriatto from whose chaps there gleamed
  A boarish tusk on either side his jaws,
With one of them the miscreant's maw unseamed.
  The mouse had fallen into cruel paws!
But Barbariccia with a fell embrace
  Grasped him, and shouted, "Stand aside: let me
Grapple him first"—Therewith he turned his face
  Towards my lord, saying, "If your will it be  64

To learn more of him, quickly make request,
　Before some other fiend the caitiff tear."
My leader then: " Say if amid the rest,
　Under the pitch, a Latian soul be there?"

The shade replied: " I left not long ago
　One that of Latium was a neighbor near;
　Ah were I with him covered deep below!
　Nor talons there nor hell-hook should I fear."　72
Then Libicocco: " We've endured too long;"
　And in the sinner's arm his weapon stuck,
　Bringing away a sinew on his prong,
　His legs, too, Draghinazzo would have struck;
But sternly round their fierce Decurion glared,
　And when their fury was a little stayed,
　My guide, without delay, of him who stared
　On his gashed limb this further question made:　80
" Whom didst thou leave — through such ill-timed desire
　To come ashore — below there as thou sayst?"
" That vessel full of all deceit, the friar
　Gomita," he replied, " Gallura's pest.
Having his master's enemies in charge,
　He served them so that each commends his love;
　For bribes, he owns, he let them go at large;
　And in his other offices above　88

No petty barterer he but prince in guile ;
  Don Michael Zanche, lord of Logodore,
  Talks with him still about Sardinia's isle,
  Of that loved theme unwearied, evermore.
O me ! look, look ! with what ferocious air
  That other demon grins: more I would say
  Did I not dread lest yonder fiend prepare,
  With his curst hook, my tettered hide to flay !"  96

Here their great General, while with eyes askant
  Fierce Farfarello seemed about to smite,
  Turned round and cried: " Malignant kite, avaunt !
  The wretch resumed, still quivering with affright,
" If ye would see or hear among this pack
  Tuscans or Lombards, I will summon such ;
  Let these Curst-claws but stand a little back,
  So that they need not fear their vengeful clutch,  104
I, sitting down here in this place with you,
  Will for myself make seven appear instead,
  Soon as I whistle, as we use to do
  Whene'er a ghost may safely raise his head."
At this Cagnazzo, wagging to and fro
  His pate and curling up his nostril, cried,
  " Hear his malicious craft, to plunge below ! "
  Then He, so rich in trickeries, replied :  112

"Yea, too malicious, seeking to obtain
  More misery for my comrades in the lake."
Here Alichin no longer could refrain,
  But raised his voice against the rest and spake :
"If thou plunge in, I'll not give chase afoot,
  But o'er the pitch my pinions I will beat;
  Come — be this bank's high screen between us put —
See if thou singly may with us compete." 120

A novel sport now, reader, shalt thou hear ;
  Soon as each fiend from that shore turned his look,
  He first of all who most had seemed austere,
The Navarrese that lucky moment took,
Set his feet firmly on the ground, and sprung
  Freed, in a moment, from their plotted toil :
  With sudden fury every devil was stung ;
But chief the fiend that caused them such a foil. 128
He sped amain, crying, "Thou'rt caught"! but slow
  His pinions proved, and little they availed
  To match the fear of him who dived below,
And back again with soaring breast he sailed.
Even thus, whene'er a falcon hovereth nigh,
  Drops the duck suddenly beneath the wave,
  Jaded and galled his foe returns on high.
Fresh rage this trick to Calcabrina gave : 136

Greedy for strife, close after him he flew,
  Glad that the ghost's escape had given him cause,
  And when the barterer vanished from his view,
  Straight in his fellow-fiend he fixed his claws.
High o'er the fosse he grappled with him fast;
  But in return the other clawed him well,
  Proving himself a powerful hawk. — At last
  Amid the boiling pitch they struggling fell. 144
The heat soon parted them: involved they sank,
  And their clogged pinions vainly strove to soar;
  But Barbariccia from the other bank
  Moaned with his mates, and sent to aid them four.
Swiftly they sped with all their hooks, and thrust
  Their prongs to rescue the entangled pair,
  Already baked within that covering crust,
  And in this fray we left 'em struggling there. 152

## CANTO THE TWENTY-THIRD.

SILENT we walked, in solitary mode,
  My master foremost and myself behind,
  As go the gray Franciscans on their road;
  While the late quarrel occupied my mind,
And to my memory that old fable came
  Touching the frog and mouse which Æsop wrote:
  Not Ay and Yea more signify the same
Than these two stories, if with careful note      8
One mark the occasion and the end of both;
  And since one thought is from another bred,
  So from that first a second had its growth,
Which brought back double all my former dread.
My trembling heart this fancy flashed across:
  These demons through our agency have met
  Discomfiture, with mockery too and loss,
Such as must needs their fiendish natures fret.      16

If rage increase that evil will of theirs,
   They will pursue us, fiercer in their spite,
   Than the fell hound the leveret which he tears:
   I felt each hair with horror stand upright.
" Master," I said, intently gazing back,
   " Unless thou quickly hide thyself and me,
   I fear from these Curst-claws a fresh attack;
   Already close behind us they must be;    24
Yea, I imagine I can feel their hooks."
   And he replied: " Were I of leaded glass,
   I could not sooner catch thine outward looks
   Than into mine thy inmost soul doth pass.
Mingling with mine this instant came thy thought,
   The same in bearing and in face as mine;
   So that of both one counsel I have wrought.
   If now this right-hand shore so much incline    32
That to the pit below we may descend,
   The imaginary chase we shall avoid."
   Of this advice he had not made an end,
   Before I saw them on their pinions buoyed:
Towards us, at no great distance, fierce they flew,
   As 'twere to strike us with their taking darts:
   Quick to himself my guide my person drew
   Even like a mother whom some outcry starts,    40

Waking, that sees the enkindled flames and wild,
   Snatches her son and flies without delay,
   Not even to catch — more caring for her child
   Than for herself — one garment on her way;
And from the summit of the flinty bank,
   Down by the pendent rock which bars one side
   Of the succeeding trench, supine he sank:
   Nor e'er did water through a conduit glide
With swifter flow to turn a land-mill's wheel,
   When to the very paddles near impelled,
   Than down that ridge my master sped with zeal,
   While on his breast my body's weight he held.
Thus bearing me as I had been his son,
   Not mere companion, scarce his feet had gained
   The bed below when those we strove to shun
   Reached the cliff o'er us — he unmoved remained.
For that high Providence which willed that they
   O'er the fifth pit in ministry preside,
   Forbids them all beyond its bounds to stray:
   Here now a painted people we descried.
Full slow, with jaded look and toilsome guise,
   They went their round with lamentable moan,
   In robes with low-hung cowls that hid their eyes,
   And shaped like those the monks wear at Cologne.

Gilded outside, with dazzling ray they glared ;
  Within, all lead, and of a load so great
  That Frederic's were of straw with these compared:
O weary mantle ! — everlasting weight !
With them together, listening their complaint,
  Still toward the left, around the chasm we kept,
  But with the burden of their vesture faint
  The weary tribe with lagging footsteps crept.   72
Thus to new spirits at each step we came :
  I asked my guide then, " May there not be found
  Some one distinguished by his deeds or name ?
  In walking with them, pray thee look around."

And one who seemed the Tuscan speech to know,
  Behind us called : " Your rapid pace restrain,
  Ye who through this murk air so swiftly go !
  From me perchance thy wish thou mayst obtain."   80
At this my leader turned and whispered, " Hold !
  Stay thy quick step and his companion be : "
  I stopped, and saw two shades whose visage told
  How eagerly they longed to be with me.
Their load and clogged path hindered their advance ;
  But, having reached us, long without a word
  With wondering eyes they looked at me askance
  Then, turning, thus together they conferred :   88

"One seems alive by motion of his throat;
 And by what privilege, if they be dead,
 Go they uncovered with the leaden coat?"
 Then thus addressing me alone they said:
"Thou to this conclave who art newly come
 Of wretched hypocrites, O Tuscan! deign
 To speak with us, nor in disdain be dumb;
 Say who thou art." I answered in this strain:
"In the great city on fair Arno's flow
 This form I wear, and always have worn, grew:
 But who are ye adown whose cheeks this woe
 Distilleth as I see such bitter dew?
What glittering pain is that wherewith ye gleam?"
 "These orange cloaks are leaden and so great
 The load thereof," one answered, "that the beam
 Of the tired balance cracks beneath the weight.

"Gay Friars we were — he Loderingo named,
 I Catalano — from Bologna's land.
 To guard her peace, your state our service claimed,
 As oft some neutral doth for umpire stand;
And for our deeds — survey Gardingo round."
 "Ye friars! your wickedness" — I thus begun,
 But said no more, beholding on the ground
 One crucified, through whom three stakes were run.

He writhed all over, seeing me, and heaved
  Beneath his beard deep sighs that spoke despair;
  And Brother Catalan who this perceived,
Said, " Yon pierced wretch on whom thou gazest there
Counselled the Pharisees to sacrifice
  One man as martyr to the people's wrath;
Now, as thou seest, his naked body lies
  Traverse forevermore across our path.
None pass but he must feel their pressure first:
  Here a like torment his wife's father rues,
  With others of that council thrice accurst,
  The seed of so much evil to the Jews."

I marked how Virgil wondering gazed the while
  On the poor wretch across the ground outspread,
  In banishment eternal and so vile.
Addressing then the friar, my master said:
" Say, if thou mayst, could our escape be made
  By any passage to the right of this,
  Without compelling those dark angels' aid
To come and guide us from this dread abyss!"
" Nearer," he answered, " than thou dar'st to hope,
  From the great circle stretching, there is bent
  O'er all these fearful pits a craggy cope;
  Only o'er this the rocky arch is rent.

Its sloping ruins ye may climb that rise
    High o'er the side and bottom of this glen."
    My guide stood looking down, in thoughtful wise,
    And said, " The fiend has misinformed us then
That yonder sinners with his weapon wrings.
    " I've at Bologna heard," replied the friar,
    " Much ill of Satan, — amid other things,
    That he's a liar, and of lies the sire."

Straightway my leader slowly onward strode,
    His face just flushed with anger's transient heat:
    I left those spirits, too, of heavy load,
    Following the print of his beloved feet.

## CANTO THE TWENTY-FOURTH.

In the year's infant season, when the sun
Tempers his tresses 'neath Aquarius' reign,
And towards the equinox the long nights run;
When the frost copies on the glittering plain
The pure, white image of her sister, snow,
Though her light writing soon is thawed away,
The peasant then, whose wintry store is low,
Starts forth and looks about him in dismay, 8
And, seeing everywhere the whitened ground,
Smites on his thigh, returning to his cot,
And wanders here and there complaining round,
Poor wretch! unknowing how to mend his lot:
Then, sallying out again, his hope revives
To see how soon the world has changed its face;
And catching up his crook, his flock he drives
To their old pasture with a cheerful pace: 16

Even so my heart sank when I marked my guide
  Wearing such trouble writ upon his brow,
  And even so soon the balsam he supplied;
For we had reached the broken causeway now;
And turning towards me with that gentle smile
  Which, at the mountain's base, I thought so sweet,
  Scanning the ruin, first he mused awhile,
Then oped his arms and raised me from my feet.  24

Like one who toiling seemeth to foresee
  Ever some other labor, still to do,
  Thus, to one fragment's top in lifting me,
Eyed he the next and cried, " Cling fast thereto!
But try it first, if 'twill thy pressure bear:"
  For a cloaked sinner 'twere no easy pass,
  Since though he bore my weight, himself but air,
Scarce could we mount from toppling mass to mass;  32
And had it not been that the encircling rim,
  On this side of the chasm, was less in height
  Than on the other, I'll not speak for him,
But for myself I had been vanquished quite.
But Malebolge sinks — its form is such —
  Still towards the mouth of the last pit of all;
  Therefore in every valley just as much
As one side rises must the other fall.  40

The ruin's topmost point at length we gained,
  Whence the last stone broke off that fell below:
  And here my lungs were of my breath so drained
  That, once arrived, I could no further go.
But as I sat, the master cried, "Arise!
  Shake off all weakness: for whoso on down,
  Or underneath a coverlet who lies,
  Never shall come to knowledge of renown:
And without fame who lets his life outwear
  Leaveth such vestige of himself behind
  As foam in water leaves or smoke in air:
  Up then! and conquer sloth by strength of mind:
The mind comes victor off in every fight,
  Unless the body burden it too much:
  Come, we have stairs to scale of loftier flight;
  'Tis not enough to have 'scaped the demons' clutch:
Profit by these words, if their sense thou heed."
  Then up I sprang, and showed myself possessed
  Of breath far better than I felt indeed,
  And said, "Lead on! I'm strong, nor wish for rest.

Now up the rock we took our way once more,
  A narrow, broken, difficult ascent,
  And steeper far than we had just climbed o'er.
  Not to seem weak, conversing still I went;

When came a voice forth from the other fosse,
  Muttering, not uttering distinctly aught:
  Though on the summit of the arch across
  I stood, the words it said I vainly sought:
But he who spake seemed full of wrath and fierce.
  I bent me to gaze down, but living sight
  That darkness could not to the bottom pierce:
  I begged my lord then to descend the height       72
To the next bank, that formed the archway's pier.
  " Yea, let us clamber down the wall," said I,
  " For as I hear, unknowing what I hear,
  So I see down but nothing can descry."
" Fulfilment is the sole reply, my son,
  I render thee: a frank request," he said,
  " Should be received in silence, and be done."
So we descended by the bridge's head,              80
  Where with the eighth bank it unites, and here
  Opened upon mine eyes the loathsome deep
  Within whose gloom I saw a sight of fear;
  Serpents of strangest kind, a horrid heap!
Remembrance in my blood a shuddering wakes.
  Let Lybia mid her sands her poisonous host,
  Chelydras, amphisbœnas, javelin-snakes,
  Chersydras, cenchris, phareas, no more boast:    88

Pests of such sort, so many and so fell,
  That country never yet produced, with all
  That in the wilds of Ethiopia dwell,
  Or o'er the deserts, by the Red Sea, crawl.

Amid this foul and savage swarm a race
  Ran trembling, naked, without hope to find
  Heliotrope's charm, or any hiding-place:
  Their hands with serpents fast were bound behind.      96
These both with head and tail their loins pierced through,
  Being in front close gathered in a knot:
  And lo! at one, beside our bank, there flew
  A reptile which transfixed him on the spot,
Striking him just where neck and shoulders blend;
  Instant the sinner kindled into flame:
  Never was O nor I more swiftly penned
  Than, sinking down, all ashes he became.      104
And soon as thus dissolved in dust he fell,
  Straightway the ashes gathered from the earth
  To their old figure: thus, great sages tell,
  The Phœnix dies, then hath a second birth,
About the term of her five hundred years,
  Through which on no green herb nor blade she feeds,
  But incense only, and the amomum's tears,
  While myrrh and spikenard form her funeral weeds.      112

As one who falls, not knowing how he falls,
  Whether some demon drag him to the ground,
  Or some obstruction that the man enthralls,
Soon as he riseth, strangely gazes round,
  And by the agony he just hath past
  Bewildered, sighs and looks with wondering stare.
Thus, as that sinner rose, he stood aghast.
  Justice of God! how terrible to bear,
That pourest down thy storm of vengeance so!
  Who he might be, my guide demanded then:
  " I rained from Tuscany, not long ago,"
Replied the wretch, "down into this wild den.
Bestial, not human life pleased me; for I
  Am Vanni Fucci, one of mulish heart:
  A beast — Pistoja was my fitting stye."
Then I to Virgil: " Bid him not depart,
  But ask what crime the caitiff hither brought;
  Whom for a man of blood and wrath I knew."
The sinner heard, nor to evade me sought,
  Though his cheeks burned with shame's distressful hue;
  But levelling at me his mind and eyes,
Gave me this answer: " More it makes me mourn
  That thou my misery shouldst thus surprise
  Than from the other life when I was torn.

I cannot choose but answer thy demand ;
Thus low I dwell because I dared invade
The sacristy's fair gifts with impious hand ;
Which deed was to another falsely laid."


" Yet to have seen me here lest thou rejoice,
When thou these pits of darkness shalt have left,
Open thine ears to my prophetic voice.              144
Pistoja first of Neri shall be reft :
Then, Florence changing both her men and laws,
Mars brings a lightning-flash from Magra's vale,
Which blackest clouds inwrap and furious flaws,
And shall ere long full bitterly assail,
In storm of battle, on Piceno's plain :
But soon the fog asunder he will tear,
Nor shall one Bianco without scath remain :        152
All which 1 tell thee to thy soul's despair.

## CANTO THE TWENTY-FIFTH.

ENDING that speech of his, the robber threw
Both hands on high, and made the sign of shame,
Crying, " God! take it — this I mean for you: "
From that time forth the snakes my friends became ;
For one, as if to say, " Blaspheme no more ! "
Entwined his neck, his arms another bound,
Then bored him through, clinching itself before,
That neither limb could stir, so tightly wound.
Ah thou Pistoja ! thou Pistoja ! why
By thine own counsels is it not decreed
That thou shouldst perish and in ashes lie,
Gone in thy guilt so far beyond thy seed ?
Through all the dingy circles down in hell
I saw no spirit 'gainst his God so proud —
Not from the walls of Thebes the wretch that fell :
He fled ; nor farther utterance was allowed.

Then I beheld a Centaur, swoln with wrath,
   Come shouting, " Where's that hardened sinner —
      where ? "
I guess Maremma fewer serpents hath
Fewer than dangling round his flanks he bare,
To where the beast and human aspect blended;
   Behind his neck and o'er his shoulders lay
   A fiery dragon, with his wings extended,
Kindling to flame all shapes that cross his way.    24
" Lo ! that is Cacus " — thus my master spake,
   " Who round his dwelling, 'neath the rocky steep
   Of Aventine, oft spread a bloody lake :
He walks not in the path his fellows keep.
For the vast herd that pastured near his cave
   He stole by trickery: great Alcides then
   Finished his frauds with mace that haply gave
A hundred strokes, though scarce felt he the ten.    32

During these words the Centaur galloped by;
   And underneath us three new spirits came
   Of whom nor Virgil was aware, nor I,
Till, " Who are ye ? " we heard the band exclaim:
This cut our story short; and for a space
   Gazing we stood, on them alone intent.
   I knew them not; but, as is oft the case,
One called another's name by accident:    40

"Ha! where is Cianfa gone?" exclaimed the shade;
   And that my guide might stand attent and hark,
   My finger straightway on my lip I laid,
   In sign of silence: now, O reader! mark,
And if my tale thou slowly shalt receive,
   Thy doubt will cause in me no great surprise;
   For I, who saw it, hardly can believe:
   But as I stared on them with lifted eyes,
Swiftly at front of one a serpent darts,
   With six feet clinging to his frame throughout;
   His fore-feet grasped the arms; the middle parts
   With his mid-feet he closely twined about.
Next with his fangs the cheeks he did assail;
   His hinder-feet he stretched o'er either thigh;
   Between them thrusting his insidious tail,
   Which up behind the loins he swung on high.
Ivy ne'er coiled about a tree so tight
   As the dread reptile his own members twined
   Around his prey; like wax, before my sight,
   Each melted into each with hues combined.
Neither appeared what he had been before:
   So, with papyrus burning, ere it fires,
   A browner color spreads the surface o'er,
   Not black as yet, although the white expires.

The others gazed, and each exclaimed: "Ah me,
   Agnello, how thou changest in thy frame!
   Nor two nor one thou seemest now to be."
Yet now a single head the two became,
   Where in one visage, which confounded two,
   The twain were blended: yea, four limbs compressed
Into two arms their lengths before my view:
   The legs and thighs, the belly and the chest, 72
Became new members, such as ne'er were seen;
   Nor of the former shape appeared a trace:
   And the perverted form, whose mingled mien
Seemed both yet neither, passed with lagging pace.

As the swift lizard, 'neath the scourging ray
   Of Dog-star time, seems lightning, if by chance,
   Flitting from hedge to hedge, it cross the way;
So did a fiery little adder glance 80
Straight at the bowels of the other two,
   A livid snake, and black as pepper's grain.
   One wretch it fastened on and stung him through,
Just there where first our nutriment is ta'en;
Then at his feet its own stretched length it cast.
   The pierced thief eyed the monster, but was dumb,
   And yawning stood with ancles planted fast,
As though by sleep or fever-fit o'ercome. 88

While on the serpent thus his gaze he bent,
  Its own the reptile on the sinner fixed ;
  One from its mouth, one from his bleeding rent
  Steamed a strong smoke that rising met and mixed.

Let Lucan now his piteous tale give o'er
  Of poor Sabellus, and Nasidius' fate,
  And list my story: Ovid now no more
  Of Arethuse and Cadmus need relate:     90
What though the poet, fabling as he wont,
  Make her a fountain, him a snakish brute;
  I envy not his art, for, front to front,
  Two natures never did he so transmute,
That each its form should for another's quit,
  As, in obedience to one law, these two:
  Into a fork the serpent's tail was split,
  The wounded shade his feet together drew.     104
His legs and thighs so closely next combined
  That of their juncture not a trace was left:
  The shape of human limbs that he resigned
  The snake's tail took, and into legs was cleft.
His skin grew hard, the snake had scales no more.
  I saw his arms within his armpits sink :
  The brute's forepaws, that had been short before,
  ' Lengthened, in manner even as those did shrink.     112

Next, the hind-feet, now close together grown,
 Became that member which mankind conceals ;
 While cloven in twain the wretch beheld his own.
 Meantime o'er both the veiling vapor steals :
This a new color gives and makes one bald,
 But on the other generates a hair ;
 One rose upright, the other grovelling crawled ;
 Yet kept those impious lamps their mutual stare, 120
Under the which each creature changed his mien ;
 For the face drew, in him that stood erect,
 Back towards the temples, where two ears were seen
 From the sleek joles' exuberance to project :
The rest thereof, which did not thus retreat,
 Into the nasal prominence arose
 And swelled the lips out, as for lips was meet :
 Meanwhile the prostrate thing puts forth its nose, 128
And even as its horns a snail draws in,
 Contracts into its head those human ears ;
 The tongue, that whole and fit for speech had been,
 Is cleft, and now a serpent's fork appears ;
The serpent's closeth, and the smoke subsides :
 The soul that had become of reptile kind .
 Speeding, with hisses, through the valley glides,
 The other sputtering human speech behind. 136
Then towards the snake the latter turned his back,

Fledged with new shoulders, and addressed the one
Who stood apart: " I crave that o'er this track
Buoso may crawl, as I before have done."

Thus did I mark the shifting ballast change
  In this seventh pit: and be my pen excused
  For wandering somewhat on a theme so strange ;
  Mine eyes were wildered and my mind confused: 144
Yet they escaped me not: I marked full well
  The limping Puccio, sole one of the three
  Comrades that came first, whom no change befell ;
  And one; Gavilla's town, made woe for thee!

## CANTO THE TWENTY-SIXTH.

Joy to thee, Florence! that so great art grown,
  Thy wings thou spreadest over shore and sea,
  And throughout Hell thy name is widely known.
  Among these thieves five such were found by me,
Children of thine in whose disgrace I share,
  And thou from them shalt no great glory gain:
  But, if our morning dreams the truth declare,
  Thou too, ere long, shalt suffer all the bane      8
That Prato prays for, not to say worse foes:
  Nay, were it now, too early 'twould not be:
  Whatever must be, would it were! — thy woes
  Will add more weight to that of years on me.

Departing hence, my guide with toilsome tread
  Up the projecting stones, which served before
  As stairs for our descent, my footsteps led,
  The crags and rocky splinters clambering o'er.      16

Pursuing thus our solitary way,
  Our feet without our hands availed us naught.
  It grieved me then, and grieves me still to-day,
  When what I saw returns upon my thought;
And with unwonted rein I hold subdued
  My genius, lest it stray from Virtue's road
  And make of none effect whatever good
  My star on me, or Heaven, may have bestowed.

As in that season when with less concealed
  A face he shines who floods the world with light,
  When to the gnat the weary fly doth yield,
  The peasant, resting on some neighbor height,
Beholds the fire-flies in the vale below,
  Wherein he ploughs, or trims his vines perchance,
  So many flames this eighth pit, all a-glow,
  Showed when its depth I fathomed with my glance.
And as whom once the avenging bears befriended
  Beheld Elijah's chariot whirled on high,
  When up to heaven the soaring steeds ascended,
  And he in vain pursued them with his eye;
Since he could only see the leaping flame,
  As heavenward, like a little cloud, it went;
  Thus through the gulf, in aspect just the same,
  Glided these fires, but hid the prey they pent:

For every flame a sinner folded in.
  I stood so bending o'er the bridge, to look,
  That I had fallen, though pushed I had not been,
  Save that such grasp of a rough crag I took.
My guide, who marked me thus intently gaze,
  Said: "In those fires the spirits are confined,
  Each in his garment of consuming blaze."
"Master," I answered, "thou confirm'st my mind:   48
Even now that thought I was about to speak;
  But who is tenant, say, of yonder fire
  That rises there with a divided peak,
  As 'twere the Theban brothers' funeral pyre?"
He answered me: "Within that martyrdom
  The great Ulysses burns, with Diomed:
  Together thus to vengeance they have come,
  As once, on earth, to wrathful deeds they sped.   56
And in their flame full bitterly they groan
  The stratagem of that famed wooden steed,
  By means whereof the gate was open thrown
  Whence issued forth the noble Roman seed.
There for that craft whence, even of life bereft,
  Deïdamia still bewails her lord,
  Her lost Achilles, yea and for the theft .
  Of Troy's Palladium they have meet reward."   64

"Master," I said, if, in that flame of theirs
　That sparkleth so, they have the power of speech,
　I pray, and pray thee with a thousand prayers,
　That thou refuse not what I now beseech.
Wait till the hornèd flame this way shall move;
　See with what eagerness I towards it bend."
"Thy prayer," he answered, " greatly I approve,
　And to thy wish a large acceptance lend.
But let thy tongue from further talk refrain;
　Leave me to parley, for I well divine
　All thy desire: they haply might disdain,
　For they were Grecians, any word of thine."
So when the flame had moved along to where
　The time and place seemed fitting to my guide,
　I heard him in this form address the pair:
　" Stay, O ye twain, that in one fire abide!
If in my life I was deserving aught,
　If much or little I deserved of you,
　When in the world my lofty verse I wrought,
　Let one his wanderings, to his death, run through."

The larger horn of that old flame began
　To curl and quiver, and a murmur woke,
　As when the wind a fluttering fire doth fan:
　Then, as it were the very tongue that spoke,

Swaying its summit to and fro, it sent
   This utterance forth: " When, for a year and more,
   Circe had held me near Gaëta pent,
Ere yet Æneas had so named the shore,
   I 'scaped her spell: but not my gentle boy,
   Nor pious reverence for mine aged sire,
Nor the due love that should have warmed with joy
   My dear Penelope, could quell the fire       9
Of my deep wish the world, and human worth,
   And human vices, too, to understand:
   But on the broad high seas I ventured forth
With one sole vessel and that little band
   Who ne'er deserted my attempt the while;
   And coasted either shore as far as Spain,
Far as Morocco, past Sardinia's isle,
   And all the rest bathed round there by the main."    104

" At last, when old and slow with life's decline,
   We reached the Strait where Hercules, of yore,
   His boundary set, in everlasting sign
That none the ocean further should explore.
   On the right hand receding Seville lay;
   On the left, Ceuta sank in ocean's breast:
Then I: ' O brothers who have stemmed your way,
   Through many thousand perils to the West!    113

To this brief vigil which remains to run
    Of your worn senses, grudge not, I entreat,
    To add the experience, following still the sun,
    Of yonder world untrod by mortal feet.
Consider, men, the seed from which ye grew!
    To live like brutes ye surely were not formed,
    But virtue still and knowledge to pursue.'
With this brief speech my comrades' minds I warmed,   120
Till for the voyage they so keenly yearned
    To hold them back I vainly had essayed;
    So to the morn our stern again was turned
    For the mad flight, and wings of oars we made.
Still towards the left our constant course we steered,
    Till night saw all the stars that spangle o'er
    The other pole, and ours no longer reared
    Its glittering host above the ocean floor."   128

Five times the moon had now renewed her ray,
    Five times the light had failed beneath her rim,
    Since first we entered on our lofty way,
    When lo! a mountain, in the distance, dim;
So high a peak before I never saw:
    We joyed, but soon our joy became lament;
    For from the new-found-land arose a flaw,
    That on our vessel's bow its fury spent.   136

Three times with all the waves it whirled us round;
At the fourth whirl the stern was lifted high,
Down went the prow — as best by Him was found!
And o'er our heads the ocean closed for aye."

## CANTO THE TWENTY-SEVENTH.

Now — for the term of its discourse was spent —
  Erect and quiet rose the steadfast flame,
  Then left us, with the gentle bard's consent;
  When lo! behind the first another came,
And by a mingled noise, therefrom that burst,
  Attracted towards its top our wondering eyes.
  Like the Sicilian bull that bellowed first,
  As just it was, with its inventor's cries,
Whose wicked file had shaped the monstrous mass,
  And by the groaning of the wretch within
  Appeared, though fashioned but of senseless brass,
  As though itself had pierced with anguish been;
Even thus, before the woful words had found
  Passage or vent, in struggling from their source,
  The fire to its own language changed the sound,
  Until they reached the summit in their course.

But to that point as soon as they had striven,
  Causing the same vibration in the peak,
  Which, on their way, the tongue within had given,
  We heard this voice: "O thou to whom I speak!
Who didst thyself, even now, use Lombard speech,
  Saying, 'Depart, I trouble thee no more;'
  Though haply somewhat late thine ear I reach,
  To speak with me have patience, I implore.  24
See, I am patient, burning as I stand:
  If thou art newly fallen to breathe the air
  Of this blind world from Latium's pleasant land,
  Whence all the burden of my sins I bear,
Tell me if now Romagna's tribes remain
  At peace, or war; for I was of the hills,
  Betwixt Urbino and the mountain chain
  Whence Tiber first unlocks his infant rills."  32

Bending I stood to listen; but my guide
  Touched my side, saying, "Speak unto him thou,
  He is Italian." Instant, I replied
  Thus, as I stood prepared to, even now:
"O hidden spirit! thy Romagna ne'er
  Was free from war, in her own tyrants' hearts;
  Nor is it now: yet, when I came from there,
  No open strife was ravaging those parts."  40

"In her old state Ravenna still abides;
  Polenta's eagle making there his nest,
  So that even Cervia with his wings he hides.
  And the brave town that stood so long a test,
And piled in bloody heaps the Frenchmen round,
  To the Green Lion's gripe at last is won.
  Verruchio's mastiffs, that Montagna found
  Such cruel keepers — both the sire and son —
Still where they wont their fangs for augurs wield:
  While, shifting sides, from midsummer to cold,
  The Lion couched upon an argent field
  Lamone's and Santerno's town doth hold:
But she whose flank is washed by Savio's flow,
  Even as her site is, in the middle way
  Betwixt the mountain and the plain below,
  Dwells between freedom and a tyrant's sway.
Now, who thou art, I pray thee frankly own:
  Be not more hard than other souls have been,
  So may thy name on earth be widely known."

The flame first roared awhile its wonted din;
Then, in its fashion, as the summit played
  From side to side, breathed to me this reply:
  " Did I believe that my response were made
  To one returning to the world on high,

This flame of mine should motionless remain:
  But since none ever did his way retrace,
  If truth I hear, from this abyss of pain,
  I give thee answer, fearing no disgrace."


" I was a soldier, then a corded friar;
  So girdled, thinking meet amends to make:
  And surely this had proved no vain desire,
  But for the Great High Priest — whom curses take!    72
'Twas he seduced me to my sins once more;
  Hear how and why, — thy hearing it is worth.
  While I my bones and pulpy members wore,
  Which my good mother gave me at my birth,
Mine was the fox's, not the lion's part:
  I knew all tricks, all covert ways of fraud;
  And with such cunning carried out their art,
  To the world's end my fame was noised abroad.    80
But when I saw that part of life begin
  Where it behoveth every man to strike
  His weary sails and take his halyards in,
  What most had pleased now bred in me dislike.
Therefore in penitence I bent my knees,
  Confessed — woe's me! — and might have grace obtained,
  But for that Prince of modern Pharisees,
  Who near the Lateran at war remained,    88

Not now with Jews nor Saracens, for all
   His foes were Christians: none amid the band
   Had ever been to conquer Acre's wall,
   Or play the merchant in the Sultan's land.
He his high office and his holy rank
   Little regarded, nor that rope of mine
   Which wont to make its fasting wearers lank.
   But in Soracte's cave as Constantine
Besought Sylvester's aid to set him free
   From leprosy, even so to get release
   From his proud fever, he consulted me
   As his physician, but I held my peace;
For scarcely sober seemed his words: 'From now
   I do absolve thee — be no more afraid' —
   He thus proceeded, 'only teach me how
   May Palestrina in the dust be laid.
Of Heaven thou know'st I hold the double keys,
   To lock and loose, by him too lightly prized
   Who went before me.' Arguments like these
   Pushed me to where some answer seemed advised:
'Father,' I said, 'the sin wherein I fall
   Since thou, I know, hast power to purge away,
   Be great in promise, in performance small —
   So shalt thou triumph in thy seat of sway.'"

" Saint Francis came my parted soul to fetch;
   But one of those black-visaged cherubs cried,
   ' Hold off your hands! nor wrong me of the wretch:
   Down he must sink, and with my slaves abide;
Yea, for the fraudulent advice he gave,
   Since which I ever at his hair have been:
   No pardon an impenitent can save,
   Nor can one both repent, yet wish to sin.        120
For contradiction will not this allow.'
   Ah wretched me! my soul what shuddering thrilled
   When, seizing me, he muttered, ' Haply thou
   Didst not believe me thus in logic skilled!'
To Minos then he hurried me, who tied
   His rigid back eight times with circling tail,
   And biting it, in his great fury, cried,
   ' This guilty wretch the stealing fire must veil!'   128
So to perdition, as thou seest, I came,
   And go with heart all rancor, clad in fire."
   Here, having ended thus, the moaning flame
   Went writhing, tossing up his pointed spire.

But we passed on, my guide and I, to where
   O'er the next moat another arch was built;
   Herein their chastisement those wretches bear
   Who, sowing discord, reaped a load of guilt.       136

## CANTO THE TWENTY-EIGHTH.

Who, even in language unrestrained by law,
   Though telling oft, could fully tell of all
   The sights of blood — the ghastly wounds I saw?
Far short of truth sure every tongue must fall:
Our mind and speech could ne'er such theme command;
   For should the multitude arise once more
   That in Apulia's many-fortuned land
(Whose battle-fields were moistened with their gore)   8
The Romans slew, and in that war so long
   In which, as Livy, the unerring, writes,
   Such spoil of rings was made, — should all the throng
That fell by Robert Guiscard and his knights,
With all whose bones even yet in heaps are found
   At Ceperàn, where each Apulian broke
   His faith, and where on Tagliacozzo's ground
Old Alard won the day, without a stroke,   16

Come back together, and should one expose
  His mangled stump, and one his limb pierced through,
  All were as nothing to the hideous woes
  Which this ninth pit presented to my view.

A cooper's vessel that by chance hath been
  Either of middle-piece or cant-piece reft,
  Gapes not so wide as one that, from his chin,
  I noticed lengthwise through his carcass cleft.  24
His entrails dangled down betwixt his thighs;
  His liver too, and that foul bag was seen
  That changeth all it gets in loathsome wise.
  And while I looked, with eager eyes and keen,
My gaze returning, with his hands he tore
  His breast, and cried: "Look, how myself I rend!
  See Mahomet mangled! he who goes before,
  Groaning and gashed, was Ali once, my friend.  32

"From chin to crown he bears a cloven face:
  And all the rest, whom thou beholdest here,
  Sowed schism and scandals in their earthly race,
  And therefore sundered go as they appear.
A fiend that cleaves us waits here at our back,
  With his fell sword renewing still the wound
  In each of this poor lacerated pack,
  When we have compassed our distressful round:

The wounds are healed ere we repass his blow.
  But who art thou, on yonder rock bemused,
  As haply to delay the destined woe
For sins whereof thyself thou hast accused?"

" Death has not reached him yet," my lord replied,
  " Nor down to torment leadeth sin his soul;
  But I, who am dead, him through Hell must guide,
From round to round, that he may know the whole:   48
This is as true as that I speak to thee."
  At this, above an hundred of the train
  Stopped in the fosse to fix their gaze on me,
Through mere amaze forgetful of their pain.

" Then tell Dolcino, thou who shortly mayst
  Behold the sun, to store his camp with food,
  (Unless down here he after me would haste)
Lest by the stress of snows he be subdued   56
And yield a triumph to Novara's race,
  Which else no light-won victory might prove."
  This word said Mahomet, with suspended pace,
Lifting one foot as if about to move;
To earth he pressed it then, nor longer stopped.
  Meanwhile another, with his gullet cleft,
  And his nose level with his eyebrows lopped,
And unto whom one only ear was left,   64

Stayed with the rest, his eyes with wonder wide
 Staring upon me, and before the rest
 Opening his throat that was all over dyed
 Vermilion, unto me these words addressed:—


" Thou whom no crime to punishment hath brought,
 And whom in Latium I have seen of old,
 Unless too strong resemblance cheat my thought,
 If e'er that gentle plain thou mayst behold          72
That from Vercelli slopes to Marcabó,
 Remember Pier da Medicina there:
 Ay, and let Fano's two best townsmen know,
 To Angiolello and Sir Guy declare,
That, if in Hell our foresight be not vain,
 Hard by Cattolica they shall be flung
 Forth from their vessel into Adria's main,
 . By a fell tyrant snared, of treacherous tongue.    80
Never did Neptune 'twixt Majorca's isle
 And that of Cyprus witness wrong like this;
 Never by pirates wrought so base a wile,
 Nor even that faithless race of Argolis.
That one-eyed traitor, he who holds in thrall
 The land which one who walketh here with me
 Would fain have never looked upon, shall call
 These two to council, making that his plea;         88

Then so contrive that neither vow nor prayer
  Shall they need further 'gainst Focára's wind."
"Show me," said I, " if thou wouldst have me bear
  Tidings of thee above, among mankind,
Who's he, in whom that sight such grief doth cause?"
  At this the sinner, seizing upon one
  Of his companions, forced apart his jaws,
  And cried: " Behold him! utterance he hath none." 96
This outcast, quelling Cæsar's doubt, declared
  That ruin ever waited on delay
  When every thing for action was prepared."

Oh, how poor Curio quivered with dismay,
His throat bereft of that perfidious tongue
  Wherewith he dared such madness to incite!
  Meanwhile one wretch, whose hands were wanting, flung
  The mangled stumps up through the lurid light, 104
Crying, as on his face their foul drops blended,
  " Give Mosca too in thy remembrance place,
  Who said, alas! 'A thing once done is ended,'
  Words that sowed trouble for the Tuscan race."
" And thine own tribe's destruction!" added I:
  With which pang heaped on pain, he strode along
  Like one to madness driven by misery.
  But I remained to gaze upon the throng, 112

And saw what I without more proof might quail
  Merely to tell, but conscience aids me here,
  The good companion that beneath the mail
  Of feeling faultless keeps men free from fear.

I truly saw, and still it haunts my view,
  A headless body, moving with like tread
  As moved the others of that mangled crew,
  And in his hand he bare his own lopt head.     120
As 'twere a lantern, dangling by the hair,
  Swinging he held it, and it cried "O me!"
  As full on me it fixed a piteous stare:
Thus his own lamp unto himself was he;
And two in one there were and one in two:
  How that can be He knows who orders thus.
And to the bridge's foot as close he drew,
  Raising his arm with all the head to us,     123
Nigh to our ears he brought these words: "O thou,
  Who walk'st, a breathing man, through Hell's abyss,
  To view the dead, behold this torment now
  And see if any be so great as this!
Know that I am — so mayst thou, as I crave,
  Bear tidings of me to the upper earth —
  Bertram de Born, the councillor who gave
  Such ill advice to John of royal birth."     136

"I put rebellion 'twixt the son and sire:
　Achitophel with more malignant art
　Did not spur Absalom to wrath, or fire
　With equal hatred kingly David's heart.
For parting those whom love did so intwine
　I bear my brain — ah! — severed from its source,
　Which yet remaineth in this trunk of mine:
　Thus retribution holds in me its course."

## CANTO THE TWENTY-NINTH.

Mine eyes were so inebriate now with grief
  At the vast numbers gashed in divers ways,
  They longed to wait and weeping, find relief.
But Virgil said: " What so attracts thy gaze?
Why stand'st thou staring fixedly below
  At yonder wretched, mutilated ghosts?
None of the other pits detained thee so.
  Consider, if thou think to count their hosts,        8
This valley two and twenty miles doth wind;
  Even now the moon beneath our feet must be:
  Our time is little that remains assigned
And more than what thou seest remains to see."
" Hadst thou observed the cause of my delay,
  When I looked down with vision so intent,
  Thou mightst have still permitted me to stay:"
I made this answer, following, as he went,        16

And added: "In that den o'er which I stood,
 Watching the crowd with so intent a stare,
 I do believe a spirit of my blood
Groans for the guilt which costs so dear down there."

The master then: "Fret not thy heart for him,
 Note something else, and let that caitiff be:
 At the bridge foot I marked him, stern and grim,
 With threatening finger fiercely point at thee. 24
I overheard them call his name, and say
 Geri del Bello: thou wast rapt so long
 With him that erst held Hautefort in his sway,
 Thou didst not heed him, and he joined his throng."
"His death by violence, my guide," said I,
 "Which to this day doth unavenged remain
 By any of his kindred shamed thereby,
 Inspired him, I suppose, with such disdain 32
That he passed by me with a silent spite;
 And all the more I pity him." With this
 We reached the first point that, with stronger light,
 Would to the bottom show the next abyss.

O'er Malebolge's final cloister here
 We stood, so all the brotherhood therein
 Might meet our gaze: strange moanings pierced mine ear,
 As arrows steeled with pity they had been. 40

I put my hands upon mine ears: such wail
  As would be heard if all the dying men
  From the pest-houses of Chiana's vale,
  And all the sick of the Maremma's fen,
And of Sardinia's isle, betwixt July
  And autumn, should be tumbled in one trench
  Howling together, such was here the cry,
  And like the smell of festering limbs the stench. 48

Descending now we reached the closing bank
  Of that long rocky bridge — still to left hand:
  Here with more vivid force my vision sank
  Down to the bottom, and the cavern scanned.
Herein the handmaid of the Most High Lord,
  Justice Infallible, requites the sin
  Of every forger she doth here record.
  And much I doubt if greater grief had been 56
To see Ægina's people all infirm,
  When so malignant was the sickly air
  That every creature, to the little worm,
  Perished, and afterwards, as bards declare,
The ancient races were restored again
  From seed of ants, than here it was to view
  The spirits languishing in that dark glen,
  Heaped round in scattered groups, a ghastly crew. 64

One o'er the shoulders of his fellow lay;
   One o'er another's belly; and a third
   Crawled on all fours along his dismal way:
   We passed them step by step, without a word,
Looking and listening to the leprous pack,
   Not one of whom could lift his feeble form;
   And two I saw there, leaning back to back,
   Propped like a pair of dishes put to warm.

O'er them from head to foot a scurvy spread:
   Nor did I ever see a groom so ply
   His currycomb, who longed to taste his bed,
   Or whose impatient lord stood waiting by,
As each full oft with his remorseless nails
   Clawed his own hide, so great a rage he felt
   Of the fell itch for which nought else avails,
   And wrenched the scabs off from his tettered pelt,
As a knife scrapeth from a bream the scales,
   Or other fish with scales of larger make.
   " O thou whose hand thy body thus unmails!"
These words to one of them my leader spake,
" Who makst a forceps of thy fingers, say
   If haply any Latian spirit lurk
   Among the rest within there, so for aye
   May thy nails last thee for this loathsome work."

"We are Italians both, whom thou seest thus
  Ravaged and raw," one wept as he replied,
  "But who art thou that hast inquired of us?"
  Then to the wretch this answer made my guide.

"I with this living man am one that go,
  From steep to steep, descending on my way,
  And him this pit of Hell I mean to show."
At this they sundered from their mutual stay,                96
And each towards me turned trembling, with the rest
  That indirectly Virgil's answer caught.
  Then my good master me alone addressed,
  Saying, "Speak to them, if thou wouldst, thy thought."

"So may your memory," then I thus began,
  "Flourish on earth for many suns, and ne'er
  By Time be stolen from out the mind of man,
  As ye your name and nation shall declare;              104
Spite of this hideous torment let me know,
  Nor dread to tell." This answer one returned:
  "Arezzo was my birthplace: Albero,
  He of Sienna, caused me to be burned;
But what I died for hath not brought me here.
  Tis true I told him, speaking but in jest,
  That I with wings my way through air could steer:
  Whereat the fool, all wonder, made request            112

That him this art of soaring I would show;
    And for no cause but that I could not make
    Of him a Dædalus, he managed so
    That his supposed sire sent me to the stake.
But me to this last cavern of the ten
    Minos, the judge who cannot err, hath doomed
    Because I practised alchemy with men."
Here turning to the poet, I resumed:     120
" Was ever nation like Sienna's vain !
    Surely the French are not so vain a tribe."

That other leper heard my taunting strain,
    And then returned this answer to my gibe.
" Save Stricca, he so frugally that spent,
    And saving Niccolo, who used the first
    The rich clove-dressing which he did invent,
In the rank garden where his kind is nurst.     128
And save the others of that spendthrift band
    'Mongst whom his wealth of vineyards and of shade
    Caccia d'Asciano scattered with light hand,
    And Abbagliato his good sense displayed.
But wouldst thou know who seconds thus the spite
    Of thy hard speech against Sienna's race,
    Sharpen thine eye and fix on me thy sight,
That thou more fairly mayst peruse my face.     13

So shalt thou see I am Capocchio's ghost.
He that by alchemy false metals made;
And if I scan thee rightly, well thou know'st
How Nature's ape right cunningly I played."

## CANTO THE THIRTIETH.

When Juno, stung through Semele, was moved
    To such a hatred of her Theban race,
    As more than one malign occasion proved,
Such frenzy fell upon King Athamas,
That he shrieked out, when once his wife he met,
    To either hand of whom an infant clung:
    "Ho! spread for yonder lioness the net,
That I may snare the mother and her young."
Then, flinging forth his pitiless claws, he took
    Little Learchus, whirled him round and round,
    And dashed the body lifeless on a rock;
While she herself and other offspring drowned.
And when harsh fortune shattered so the pride,
    Which dared do all things, of the Trojan race,
    That with their king their kingdom also died;
Hecuba, widowed, captive, in disgrace,

After that her Polyxena in gore
  She had beheld, and, grief-worn mother! marked
  Her Polydorus dead upon the shore,
  Mad with her misery, like a mastiff barked;
(Such power had anguish to distort her mind)
  But furies, Theban or of Troy, nor then
  Nor were seen ever in so fell a kind,
  Goading even beasts, much less the limbs of men,  24
As in two ghosts that I saw rushing by,
  Naked and pale, and snapping as they sprang,
  Mad as a boar-pig shut out from the stye.
  One in Capocchio's neck-joint stuck his fang,
Dragging him down, until his belly grated
  The solid bottom, while the Aretine
  Exclaimed to me, as trembling he awaited,
  " Yon sprite's Gian Schicchi; with such frenzied mien  32
He rages round, assaulting this poor pack."
  " Oh!" answered I; " have patience yet, I pray,
  So may its teeth have mercy on thy back,
  Who is yon other? ere it vanish, say."

And he to me: " Thou seest the ancient shade
  Of sinful Myrrha, one that overwarm
  With love, not filial, for her father, made
  Wanton with him, in counterfeited form;  40

Even as yon other, that he might obtain
   The lady of the herd, with wicked skill
   Buoso Donati's person dared to feign,
Fixing a false seal to a forgèd will."
And when that furious pair had passed along
   Whom I had kept mine eye so bent on seeing,
   I turned its gaze to note the following throng
Of ill-born wretches, and beheld a being
Shaped like a lute, had but the groin been cleft
   From his forked portion. Dropsy's heavy woe,
   By which our human members are bereft,
Through perverse humors, of proportion so
That none betwixt the face and paunch remains,
   Forced him to keep his parching lips asunder,
   As hectic sufferers do, whom thirst constrains
To lift the upper one, and drop the under.

" O ye that stand there! and I know not why,
   Without a penance, in this world of gloom,"
   He said to us, " give heed with ear and eye
To Master Adam's miserable doom :
On earth of all I wished I had my fill,
   And now, alas! one drop of water crave.
   The little brooks that every verdurous hill
Of Casentino pours to Arno's wave,

Freshening the soft, cool channels where they glide,
  Still haunt my vision, nor in vain do haunt;
  Far more by their dear image I am dried
Than by this drouth which makes my visage gaunt.
Stern Justice thus doth rigidly devise
  That the same place wherein I sinned should be
  The occasion still of never-ceasing sighs:
For there Romena stands — dread name for me!  72
'Twas there I falsified the metal's worth
  On which the Baptist's impress had been made,
  Wherefore I left my body burned on earth:
But might I see down here the suffering shade
Of Alexander, or the County Guy,
  Ay, or their brother's, I'd not give that sight
  For all the drink Fount Branda could supply.
One is already in this woful plight,
If these mad shadows that go raging round,
  Amid their fury, can the truth relate:
  But what avails it me with limbs thus bound?
Were I so light that I could drag my weight
An inch a century, I had, ere this,
  Hunted him out amid this shapeless brood,
  Though eleven miles this pit wind round the abyss,
Nor less than half a mile of width include.

'Tis through their means that I'm with such a race:
  They tempted me to coin those florins fair
  Which with three carats of alloy were base."
And I to him: "Who are yon grovelling pair
At thy right hand there, steaming on the ground,
  Like a wet hand in winter?" He replied:
  "When I rained down here, those two souls I found;
  And since that time they motionless abide.
Nor shall they stir, I guess, for evermore.
  Sinon from Troy is one, that faithless Greek;
  And one false witness against Joseph bore:
'Tis the sharp fever makes them so to reek."

The former then, as though his name to hear
  Vilified thus, enraged he had become,
  Struck the swoln belly with a fist severe,
  That made it vibrate, ringing like a drum.
But Master Adam at his visage straight
  Aimed back the blow, with arm that seemed as hard,
  Saying, "What though these members by their weight
  Are from all faculty of motion barred,
I have an arm yet free for such a use."
  "Ah!" the Greek answered, "when thou wast conveyed
  Bound to the stake, thy hands were not so loose;
  Though free enough when those bad coins they made."

"Thou speakst more true," the dropsied wretch replies,
    Than when they bade thee tell the truth at Troy."
"Well," answered Sinon, "if I uttered lies,
    Uttering false monies was thy base employ;
And for one falsehood I am here indeed,
    But thou for more than any fiend in Hell."


"Bethink thee, perjurer, of thy wooden steed!
    The gross one cried — " the world knows that trick well:
Be that thy torment!" — " Be thine own the drout,"       121
    Returned the Greek, "which thy cracked tongue so dries,
    And the rank liquid that so swells thee out,
    Making that paunch a hedge before thine eyes."
" Still, as of old, wide gapes thy ready jaw
    To give malignant words," the coiner said;
" If I have thirst, if moisture bloat my maw,
    Thine is the burning, thine the anguished head.       128
Nay, and to lick Narcissus' mirror dry
    But little urging wouldst thou need, I trow."


Thus jangled they, while I stood waiting by,
    Until the master said: " Keep staring now!
A little more and we shall quarrel too."
    Soon as I felt that he with anger spake,
    Towards him I turned with so much shame, that through
    My memory still disturbance it doth wake.       136

And like a man who dreams of some hard lot,
   And dreaming, wishes it were but a dream,
   And so desires what is as though 'twere not,
   Thus in my dumb confusion did I seem:
Seeking excuse, I found the excuse I sought,
   Yet knew it not. The master then to me:
   " To greater fault less shame had pardon brought;
   So from all sadness have thy spirit free;     144
And, if chance e'er again thy footsteps guide
   Where in like manner men display their ire,
   Remember I am ever at thy side:
   To list such wrangling is a low desire."

## CANTO THE THIRTY-FIRST.

The tongue that flushed my cheeks with so severe
   A reprimand, a healing balm conveyed.
   Thus, I am told, could the paternal spear
Of great Achilles cure the wound it made.
Now from that woful vale we turned away,
   Crossing the bank that girds it, without speech.
   Here less it was than night, and less than day,
So that not far my visual power could reach:   8
But the deep note of a loud-pealing horn,
   Such as had even the loudest thunder drowned,
   In the direction whence the peal was borne,
Drew my intent eyes following towards the sound.
So dread a blast Orlando did not blow,
   After the doleful rout, when Charlemagne
   Met in his holy enterprise o'erthrow.
Looking a little up towards that harsh strain,   16

Many tall towers methought I could descry:
  "Master," I asked, "what sort of town is this?"
  He answered me: "The distance which thine eye
  Travels in darkness makes thy sight amiss:
Therefore thy fancy runs a little wild.
  Thou shalt see well, if thou approach the place,
  How much the eye by distance is beguiled:
  Now then, a little onward prick thy pace."    24

Tenderly then he took my hand, and, "Here,"
  Continued he, "ere further we have gone,
  Know, that the fact less startling may appear,
  Giants, not towers, are those thou gazest on.
There in the central well are all immersed,
  Each from his navel down, about the bank."
  As when a fog breaks, ere it be dispersed,
  Little by little from the dark and dank    32
The sight shapes out those objects hid before;
  Thus piercing that gross air, and getting near
  And nearer still to the surrounding shore,
  Mine error fled, but instant grew my fear.

As Montereggion stands with turrets crowned
  About its circuit, thus these giants grim,
  Towering with half their persons, rose around
  And overtopped the pit's encircling rim.    40

These are the fiends at whom Jove still doth launch
  Threats when he thunders. I already traced
  The face of one, great portion of his paunch,
  Shoulders and breast, and arms adown his waist.
Sure Nature, when her hand forebore the skill
  To make such monsters, had a wise intent,
  Taking from Mars those ministers of ill;
  And if she do not of her whales repent
And elephants, who closely thinks, will find
  That she herein a just discretion shows:
  For were ill will and strength gifted with mind,
  Vainly would men such argument oppose.
As long and large a visage he upreared
  As is Saint Peter's pine at Rome; and such
  His other bones proportionedly appeared:
  Since from the bank, that girt his waist, so much
Of his vast form was visible, that three
  Tall Frieslanders could not have reached his hair:
  Thirty good palms of him mine eye could see,
  Below where men their cloak-clasps use to wear.

" *Ràpheghi màhameth ìzabig halmi*" — thus
  The savage mouth, which hymns of sweeter note
  Would ill agree with, straight saluted us.
  " Fool," said my leader, " hush thy clamorous throat!

Soul of confusion! with thy horn alone
   Give thy wrath vent — that brays thy passion best:
   Search on thy neck there, thou wilt find the zone
   That binds it dangling round thy giant breast."
Then thus to me: " The slave is self-accused;
   Nimrod that is, to whose bad thought is due
   That in the world one language is not used;
   There let him stand, nor vain discourse pursue: 72
For every language is to him a sound,
   Like his to others, jargon without sense."
   So leftward turned, a bowshot on we found
   Another, far more fierce, of size immense.

What master-hand had power those limbs to bind
   I cannot say; but both his arms were fast,
   The left before him, and the right behind,
   Held by a chain which round his form was cast. 80
From his neck down, five circles of the chain
   Were plain to view. "That haughty spirit strove,"
   My leader said, " and so deserves his pain,
   To match his might against the most high Jove.
'Tis Ephialtes; great his exploits were,
   When giant rebels filled the Gods with dread:
   But those huge arms he nevermore shall stir."
   " Master, if it were possible," I said, 88

"The measureless Briareus I would see."
  He answered thus: "Antæus, if thou wilt,
  Thou mayst behold; he speaks — his limbs are free,
  He shall convey us to the depths of guilt.
Near us he stands: the other one, for whom
  Thou hast inquired, is yonder distant far,
  Fettered like this one, by an equal doom;
  But still more terrible his features are."
Never did earthquake, with so violent shock,
  Strongly and suddenly, a turret shake
  As Ephialtes 'gan to reel and rock;
  Nor e'er did I with fear of death so quake:
Save that I saw the bonds that held him fast,
  Terror alone had slain me on the spot;
  But now we reached Antæus, towering vast,
  Without the head, full five ells forth his grot.

"O thou that, in the vale where fortune led
  Scipio to glory — when in such dismay
  Great Hannibal, with all his heroes, fled —
  Didst bear a thousand lions for thy prey!
Through whose assistance, hadst thou only striven,
  Leagued with thy brothers, in the lofty fray,
  Many there be who think, despite of Heaven
  That Earth's proud children might have won the day!

Be now our convoy, nor disdain the task,
   Where the numb winter locks Cocytus flow.
   Bid us nor Tityos, nor Typhœus ask ;
   What here you crave, this mortal can bestow.
Stoop then, nor curl thy nostril in disdain :
   To sound thy fame on earth still, he hath power ;
   He lives, and long time living will remain,
   Unless to her Grace call him, ere his hour.   120

The monster straight — as thus the master-bard —
   Stretched his huge hands forth, and my leader clasped,
   Those hands that erst wrung Hercules full hard.
   And Virgil, when he felt himself thus grasped,
Said, " Hither ! let mine arms thy form enclose : "
   Thus we became one burden, he and I.
   And as the tower of Carisenda shows
   To one beneath it, if a cloud go by,   128
So that the tower hangs adverse to the cloud ;
   Such looked Antæus, watching as I stood
   To see him bend ; and, as his figure bowed,
   I would have fain some other way pursued.
But at the base of the devouring den,
   Where Judas lies with Lucifer, at last
   He lightly set us down, and straight again
   Lifted himself up, like a vessel's mast.   136

## CANTO THE THIRTY-SECOND.

Had I rhymes harsh and rude enough in sound,
  To suit the nature of the dismal den
  Which all the rocks hang buttressing around,
  My full conceit should have expression then;
But lacking these, I fear my speech is faint;
  For 'tis no task wherewith to be amused,
  The bottom of the universe to paint,
  Nor for a tongue to infant lispings used.
But may those virgins make my verse exact,
  Who helped Amphion build his Theban wall,
  And give me utterance not below the fact.
  And, O ye wretches! most ill-starred of all,
Of whose abode 'tis terrible to tell,
  Better had you been goats on earth or sheep!
  Being now down, within the gloomy well,
  Under the giant's feet, but far more deep,

And while the lofty wall I still admired,
    I heard this voice : " Be careful of thy tread !
    Let not thy trampling soles offend these tired,
Sad brethren here, nor bruise them on the head."
Turning whereat, beneath me and before,
    I saw a lake that seemed to be of glass
    Rather than water — so 'twas frozen o'er.
Never did winter with so gross a mass
Veil Austrian Danube, or the river Don,
    There under that cold sky : had Tambernich
    Or Pietrapana's mountain fallen thereon,
Not even its rim had creaked, it lay so thick.
And as a frog squats croaking from a stream,
    With nose put forth, what time the village maid
    Oft in her slumber doth of gleaning dream,
Stood in the ice there every doleful shade.
Livid as far as where shame paints the cheek,
    And doomed their faces downward still to hold,
    Chattering like storks, their weeping eyes bespeak
Their aching hearts, their mouths the biting cold.

I looked around me for awhile ; then fixed
    My gaze below, on two just under us,
    So linked together that their hairs were mixed.
" O ye," said I, " who breast each other thus !

Tell who ye are:" Hereat their necks they bent;
And looking up, as they their faces showed,
Their eyes, in which the moisture had been pent,
Dropped icy tears which down their lips o'erflowed.
These freezing straight, their eyelids closely shut:
Never were planks by clamp so closely held;
Whence they, like two he-goats, began to butt
Each other blindly, by such wrath compelled. 48
And one whose ears the frost had gnawed away,
Still hanging down his countenance, exclaimed
"Why dost thou eye us with that sharp survey?
Know (if thou'rt wondering how those two are named)
The vale, from which Bisenzio's water runs
Down into Arno, once belonged to them
And Count Alberto — for they were his sons,
And both were issue of a single stem. 56
Thou shalt not find, search all Caina through,
One soul more worthy in this ice to stand,
Not even that wretch whom royal Arthur slew,
Body and shadow piercing with one brand:
No, nor Focaccia, nor this other ghost
That with his head obstructeth so my sight:
If thou'rt a Tuscan, him full well thou knowst;
For Sassol Mascheroni was he hight. 64

And I, that thou mayst further question spare,
  Am Camicione, waiting to behold
  Carlin, whose guilt shall make my foulness fair."

A thousand visages I saw, by cold
Turned to dog-faces: horror chills me through
  Whenever of those frozen fords I think.
  And as we nearer to the centre drew,
  Towards which all bodies by their weight must sink,   72
There, as I shivered in the eternal chill,
  Trampling among the heads, it happed, by luck,
  Or destiny — or, it may be, my will —
  Hard in the face of one my foot I struck.
Weeping he cried, " What brings thee bruising us ?
  Unless on me fresh vengeance thou wouldst pile
  For Mont' Aperti, why torment me thus ?"
  And I: " My Master, wait for me awhile,   80
That I through him may set one doubt at rest ;
  Then, if thou bid me hasten on, I will."
  My leader stopped ; and I the shade addressed
  Who kept full bitterly blaspheming still,
" Say who art thou whose tongue so foully speaks ?"
  " Nay, who art thou that walkst the withering air
  Of Antenora, smiting others' cheeks
  That, wert thou living, 'twere too much to bear ?"   88

"Living I am; and thou, if craving fame,
    Mayst count it precious," this was my reply,
    "That I with other notes record thy name."
He answered thus: " Far other wish have I.
Trouble me now no longer — get thee gone:
    Thine is cold flattery in this waste of Hell."
At this his hindmost hairs I fastened on,
    And cried, " Thy name! I'll force thee now to tell,    96
Or not one hair upon thy head shall grow."
    He answered thus: " Although thou pluck me bare,
    I'll neither tell my name, nor visage show;
Nay, though a thousand times thou rend my hair."

I held his tresses in my fingers wound,
    And more than one tuft had I twitched away
    As he, with eyes bent down, howled like a hound;
When one cried out, " What ails thee, Bocca? say —    104
Canst thou not make enough clack with thy jaws,
    But thou must bark too? What fiend pricks thee now?"
    " Aha!" said I, " henceforth I have no cause
To bid thee speak, thou cursed traitor thou!
I'll shame thee, bearing truth of thee to men."
    " Away!" he answered: " what thou wilt, relate;
    But, shouldst thou get from hence with breath again,
Mention him too so ready with his prate.    112

Here he bewails that silver of the French:
   I saw Duera's lord, thou mayst declare,
   Down where the sinners in the coolness blench.
And if thou'rt asked what other souls were there,
Beside thee Beccarìa stands, whose throat
   Florence did cut.  Beyond, Soldànier's shade,
   And Ganellon, and Tribaldello note,
Who, when Faenza slept, her gates betrayed."    120

Him had we left, when, in a single gap,
   Fast froze together other two I saw,
   So that one head was its companion's cap:
And as a famished man a crust might gnaw,
So gnawed the upper one the wretch beneath,
   Just where the neck-bone's marrow joins the brain:
   Not otherwise did Tydeus fix his teeth
On Menalippus' temples in disdain.    128
While thus he mumbled skull and hair and all,
   I cried: "Ho! thou who showst such bestial hate
   Of him on whom thy ravenous teeth so fall,
Why feedst thou thus? on this agreement state;
That, if thou have good reason for thy spite,
   Knowing you both, and what his crime was, I
   Up in the world above may do thee right,
Unless the tongue I talk with first grow dry."    136

## CANTO THE THIRTY-THIRD.

From his foul feast that sinner raised his jaw,
   Wiping it on the hair, first, of the head
   Whose hinder part his craunching had made raw.
Then thus, " Thou wouldst that I renew," he said,
" The agony which still my heart doth wring,
   In thought even, ere a syllable I say;
   But if my words may future harvest bring
To the vile traitor here on whom I prey                6
Of infamy, then thou shalt hear me speak,
   And see my tears too. I know not thy mien,
   Nor by what means this region thou dost seek ;
But by thy tongue thou'rt sure a Florentine.

Know then, Count Ugolino once was I,
   And this Archbishop Ruggieri : fate
   Makes us close neighbors — I will tell thee why.
'Tis needless all the story to relate,                  16

How through his malice, trusting in his word,
   I was a prisoner made and after slain.
   But that whereof thou never canst have heard,
   I mean how cruelly my life was ta'en,
Thou shalt hear now, and thenceforth know if he
   Have done me wrong.           A loophole in the mew
   Which hath its name of Famine's Tower from me,
   And where his doom some other yet must rue,     24
Had shown me now already through its cleft
   Moon after moon, when that ill dream I dreamed
   Which from futurity the curtain reft.
He, in my vision, lord and master seemed,
   Hunting the wolf and wolfcubs on the height
   Which screeneth Luccá from the Pisan's eye:
With eager hounds, well-trained and lean and light,
   Gualandi and Lanfranchi darted by,     32
With keen Sismondi — these the foremost went;
   But after some brief chase, too hardly borne,
   The sire and offspring seemed entirely spent,
   And by sharp fangs their bleeding sides were torn."

" When, before morn, from sleep I raised my head,
   I heard my boys, in prison there with me,
   Moaning in slumber and demanding bread.
   If thou weep not, a savage thou must be:     40

Nay, if thou weep not, thinking of the fear
　My heart foreboded, canst thou weep at aught?
　Now they woke also, and the hour was near
　When used our daily pittance to be brought.
His dream made each mistrustful; and I heard
　The door of that dread tower nailed up below:
　Then in my children's eyes, without a word,
　I gazed, but moved not; and I wept not: so　　48
Like stone I was within, that I could not.
　They wept though, and my little Anselm cried,
　'Thou lookst so, Father! what's the matter, what?'
　But still I wept not, nor a word replied
All that long day, nor all the following night,
　Till earth beheld the sun's returning ray;
　And soon as one faint gleam of morning light
　Stole to the dismal dungeon where we lay,　　56
And soon as those four visages I saw
　Imaging back the horror of mine own,
　Both hands through anguish I began to gnaw;
　And they, believing want of food alone
Compelled me, started up and cried, 'Far less,
　Dear Father, it will torture us if thou
　Shouldst feed on us! thou gavest us this dress
　Of wretched flesh — 'tis thine, and take it now.　　64

So, to relieve their little hearts, at last
   I calmed myself, and, all in silence thus,
   That and the next day motionless we past —
   Ah, thou hard earth! why didst not ope for us?

On the fourth morning, Gaddo at my feet
   Cast himself prostrate, murmuring, 'Father! why
   Dost thou not help me? give me food to eat.'
   With that he died: and even so saw I,
As thou seest me now, three more, one by one,
   Betwixt the fifth day and the sixth day fall;
   By which time, sightless grown, o'er each dear son
   I groped, and two days on the dead did call:
But, what grief could not do, hunger did then."
   This said, he rolled his eyes askance, and fell
   To gnaw the skull with greedy teeth again,
   Strong as a dog's upon the bony shell.

Ah Pisa! shame of all in that fair land
   Where *si* is uttered, since thy neighbors round
   Take vengeance on thee with a tardy hand,
   Broke be Capraja's and Gorgona's bound!
Let them dam Arno's mouth up, till the wave
   Whelm every soul of thine in its o'erflow!
   What though *'twas said* Count Ugolino gave,
   Through treachery, thy strongholds to the foe,

Thou needst not have tormented so his sons,
   Thou modern Thebes! their youth saved them from
     blame—
Brigata, Hugh, and those two innocent ones
   Whom, just above, the canto calls by name.

We now passed on, to where another race
   In the rough bondage of the frost is pent,
Hanging not down, but holding up the face,
   Whose very weeping weeping doth prevent.     96
The tears, which at their eyes a barrier find,
   Are forced within to make their anguish more;
For the first drops clog those that come behind,
   The cup with crystal visor glazing o'er.
And though no longer much sensation dwelt
   In my own visage, callous from the cold,
Methought a breeze upon my cheek I felt,
   And of my master would the cause be told.     104
"Is not all wind," I said, "spent here below?"
He answered: "Fast thou art approaching where
Thy very eye the meet response will show,
   Seeing the source which poureth such an air."
And one of those sad souls in that cold crust
   Cried: "O ye spirits of so cruel kind,
That to the lowest region ye are thrust!
   These frozen curtains from mine eyes unbind;     112

Let me a little vent this bursting heart,
   Before again my gathering tears congeal."
   I answered him: "First tell me who thou art,
   If thou wouldst have me those glazed orbs unseal;
And if I free thee not, may I be sunk
   Down to the bottom of this ice!" "My name,
   The wretch replied, "is Alberic the monk;
   I'm he whose fruit from no good garden came:     120
Now for those figs of mine I get this date."

"What! art thou dead then?" I exclaimed; and he
   Answered me thus: "I know not in what state
   My body in the upper world may be.
This one advantage beareth over all
   The rest of Hell our Ptolemæan part,
   That oft the soul is hither doomed to fall
   Ere Atropos compel its final start.     128
That thou more willingly mayst rub away
   These frozen drops that overglaze my face,
   Learn that no sooner doth a soul betray,
   As I did, than a demon takes its place,
Who rules the body till its term be run,
   While to this cistern here the soul is hurled:
   Even now perchance the body of this one,
   Who winters here behind me, walks the world.     136

If thou but newly art descended here,
　His outward semblance haply thou mayst know:
　That's Master Branca Doria; many a year
　Hath glided by since he was chained below."

" Now I believe thou'rt mocking me," said I;
　" For Branca Doria surely hath not gone
　To his grave yet, but in the world on high
Eats, drinks and sleeps and putteth raiment on."
" Ere to the fosse of those Curst-Claws," he said,
　" Up where the pitch boils, Michel Zanche came,
　This caitiff left a devil in his stead,
Yea, in his own and in a kinsman's frame,
One who shared with him in his traitorous plot.
　But put thy hand forth now and let me see;
　Open mine eyelids ! " — and I oped them not:.
Rudeness was courtesy to such as he.

Ah Genoese! men wanting in all worth,
　With every taint of wickedness accurst,
　Why are ye not swept off the face of earth?
Seeing that with this spirit, far the worst
Even of Romagna, one of you I found
　Who, for his eminence in works of ill,
　Hath his soul down there in Cocytus drowned,
　Yet seems, above, alive in body still.

## CANTO THE THIRTY-FOURTH.

" *Vexilla Regis prodeunt Inferni* —
   The flags are flying of the King of Hell!
   Towards us they wave: so, look " — the master said —
" Before thee now, if thou see Him as well."
As when a thick fog all things hath o'erspread,
   Or darkness veils our hemisphere, oft shows
   A mill far off whose wheels by wind are sped,
   Appeared a frame in front of me that rose.     8
Then, finding from the blast that swept along
   No shelter else, behind my guide I shrunk
   And saw — with fear I set it in my song —
   That, where I was, the shades were wholly sunk.
Through the clear ice their forms were plain to sight,
   Like splints in glass, erect, or lying low,
   One with soles up, and one with head upright,
   Another, face to foot, bent like a bow.     16

Soon as my lord had led me on to where
  His pleasure 'twas to point to my survey
  The being that was once, outside, so fair,
  He from before me passed, and bade me stay.
" Lo, Dis ! " he said, " and lo, the place where thou
  Hast need to arm thy soul with all its might ! "
  How frozen I became, how helpless now,
  Ask me not, reader — 'tis not mine to write ;    24
And forms of speech would all too trivial be :
  I was not dead, yet scarce alive remained :
  Think for thyself, if genius bloom in thee,
  What my state was, whom neither state contained.

At mid-breast, rising from the ice, on high
  He towered who sways that empire of despair ;
  And more my size might with a giant's vie
  Than giants could with even his arms compare :    32
Judge what the whole must be of such a part !
  If, once as beauteous as he now is grim,
  He on his Maker scowled in scorn of heart,
  Well may all miseries have their source in him.

Oh, what a marvel it appeared to me,
  When I beheld upon the monster's head
  More than one countenance ! — for he had three :
  One face he bare in front, and that was red.    40

The other twain, that did with this unite,
    Just o'er the middle of each shoulder grew,
    Combining where his crest had place; the right
    Was mingled white and yellow in its hue;
The left was such in color as the race
    Wear, of that land whence Nile sends down his stream.
    Two mighty pinions rose from 'neath each face,
    Such as might best so huge a fowl beseem;     48
Plumes had they none, but more like bat than bird;
    Sails on the sea I never saw like those;
    And these he flapped, and so to motion stirred
    Three winds, whose fanning all Cocytus froze.
A bloody slaver down his triple chin
    Flowed, mixed with tears, from those six eyes that came;
    And in each mouth, as 'twere his teeth had been
    A sort of brake, he champed a sinner's frame:     56
Thus three he held in his tormenting clutch.
    To him in front, the biting, if compared
    With the ferocious clawing, was not much;
    For oft his back of skin was wholly bared.

"That foremost soul up there," the master said,
    "Whose limbs are quivering with intenser pain,
    Is Judas, called Iscariot: see! his head
    Inside he hath, outside his legs remain.     64

Brutus is one of those, with heads down-hung,
Dangling from that black jaw: take note of him,
How he doth wring! yet silence chains his tongue:
Cassius that other is, more large of limb.
But the night cometh up again ; and now
We must depart: we have seen every thing."


His neck I girdled then (he teaching how)
While he chose time and place, when every wing         72
Was on the stretch: when they were wide enough,
Grasping the woolly ribs, from lock to lock
He clambered down, betwixt the creature's rough
Thick-matted tufts and that ice-crusted rock.
When we had reached the swelling of the joint
Where turns the thigh, my leader, struggling sore,
Turned round with pains, precisely at this point,
His head to where his feet had been before ;         80
And as he grappled hard the shaggy hairs,
(Like a man climbing) back to Hell, methought,
I was returning.  " Take fast hold! such stairs,"
The master gasped, like one with toil o'erwrought,
" Must serve us now, such wickedness to quit."
Then through an opening in a rock he passed,
And placing me upon its brink to sit,
With caution moved, and stopped near me at last.       88

I raised mine eyes, expecting still to see
  Lucifer, just as I had left him there,
  Standing erect; and he appeared to me
  Inverted, with his legs up in the air.

Then if confusion struck me not aghast,
  The multitude may guess, whose grosser eyes
  Heed not what point it is I just had passed.
" Now," said the master, " to thy feet arise :
Long is the journey, and the way not good ;
  Towards his third hour the sun hath halfway risen."
  No corridor it was, wherein we stood,
  Of some fair palace, but a natural prison ;
Its ground was craggy, and it wanted light;
  And, " O my master ! ere from this abyss
  I make escape," said I, when once upright,
  " Draw me from error first, and tell me this :
Where is the ice? and this huge figure — how
  Comes he reversed thus strangely? and the sun —
  How happeneth it that he already now
  From night to morning hath his journey run."

He answered thus : " Thou fanciest thou art still
  That side the centre, where I grasped the hair
  Of the Bad Worm that bores through earth with ill.
  While I descended, thou indeed wast there :

But when I turned, the central point we passed
   Towards which all weights draw, from on every hand:
   Thou'rt under now this hemisphere whose vast
   Opposes that covering the great dry land,
Beneath whose zenith, suffering for your sakes,
   The Sinless Born without sin lived and died.
   Thy feet are on a lesser sphere which makes
   Of the Giudecca's base the outer side.    120
'Tis morning here when there the sun hath set:
   And he, the shaggy ladder of our way,
   Fixed, as he fell from heaven, abideth yet.
   This side he fell: the land then, in dismay,
Though erst projecting, sought your hemisphere,
   And sank in ocean: him perchance to fly,
   Whatever now doth on this side appear
   Left here this void, and trembling rushed on high."    128


A place there is 'neath Beelzebub extending
   Far as his tomb is deep; unseen, but known
   By the low murmur of a rill descending
   A chasm its course hath gnawed out in the stone,
Falling not much, but winding as it flows;
   Into which secret way my guide and I
   Entered to pass, not caring for repose,
   Back to the beautiful, bright world on high,    136

And clambered up, he ever leading on,
Until heaven's lovely things, within my ken,
Through a round opening in the cavern shone ;
And thence we rose to see the stars again.

END OF THE INFERNÓ

OF

DANTE ALIGHIERI.

*Tantus labor non sit cassus!*

www.ingramcontent.com/pod-product-compliance
Lightning Source LLC
Chambersburg PA
CBHW031826230426
43669CB00009B/1233